LISTENING
WITH

My
HEART

LISTENING
WITH
MY
HEART

by

Heather Whitestone

with

Angela Elwell Hunt

GALILEE
DOUBLEDAY
NEW YORK LONDON TORONTO SYDNEY AUCKLAND

A GALILEE BOOK
PUBLISHED BY DOUBLEDAY
a division of Bantam Doubleday Dell Publishing Group, Inc.
1540 Broadway, New York, New York 10036

GALILEE, DOUBLEDAY, and the portrayal of a ship with a cross above a book are trademarks of
Doubleday, a division of Bantam Doubleday Dell Publishing Group, Inc.

First Galilee edition published July 1998 by special arrangement with Doubleday.

Lyrics from "Listen to Your Heart" by Deborah Craig-Claar and Mark Hayes
© 1996 PILOT POINT MUSIC (Administered by the COPYRIGHT COMPANY,
Nashville, TN). All Rights Reserved. International Copyright Secured. Used By Permission.

Text design by Stanley S. Drate/Folio Graphics Co., Inc.

The Library of Congress has cataloged the Doubleday hardcover edition as follows:

Whitestone, Heather.
     Listening with my heart / by Heather Whitestone with Angela Elwell
Hunt.—1st ed.
        p.   cm.
     Summary: The first physically handicapped woman to win the Miss
America Pageant tells the story of her deafness, love of ballet,
education, and challenge to fulfill her God-given potential.
     1. Whitestone, Heather—Juvenile literature.   2. Beauty
contestants—United States—Biography—Juvenile literature.   3. Deaf
women—United States—Biography—Juvenile literature.   4. Miss
America Pageant, Atlantic City, N.J.—Juvenile literature.
     [1. Whitestone, Heather.   2. Beauty contestants.   3. Deaf.
4. Physically handicapped.   5. Women—Biography.   6. Miss
America
Pageant, Atlantic City, N.J.]   I. Hunt, Angela Elwell, 1957–
II. Title.
     HQ1220.U5W45   1997
     791.6'2—dc21
     [B]   97-906
                                                                       CIP
                                                                       AC

Heavenly Father, this book is for you. You have taught me so much through other people's lives.

For the joys, the trials, and the uphill path, I thank you.

I also owe a world of thanks to the Miss America Pageant volunteers, my teachers, my friends, and most of all, my husband and my family.

Listen to Your Heart

BY DEBORAH CRAIG-CLAAR AND MARK HAYES

You listened to your heart.
You heard a different song.
A deeper, truer voice that said you had a choice
To bend to the wind or be strong.
So you chose a distant road
And you left behind your fears,
For when your heart belongs to God . . . and you listen . . .
His voice is what you'll hear.

Some roads are always steep,
But worthy of the climb.
Journeys demand patience,
Patience begs for time.

Just listen to your heart.
You'll always hear that song,
That deeper, truer voice that says you have a choice
To follow your dreams all along . . .
And if you trust your heart to God . . . and then listen . . .
His voice is all you'll hear.

Contents

LISTENING
WITH
MY
HEART

1 Caught by Surprise

Sometimes life catches us by surprise.

Sometimes, though, those surprises are hinted at in our dreams.

Consider David, the shepherd boy who went to check on his big brothers who were in the Israelite camp. Imagine his distress when he arrived and discovered that the entire army of hundreds of strong men had been sidelined—by a single boastful giant! David was so young and so small that a man's armor hung from his slender frame, more an encumbrance than protection. With five simple stones, the best weapons he knew, he went out in the name of God, killed the giant, and brought peace to the land. David, the one who praised God through his dance, had faith in his dream . . . and in his God.

Barely twenty years ago, in a little Alabama town, a deaf girl dreamed of dancing ballet before an adoring crowd to music she couldn't hear . . . and receiving a crown for her efforts. On September 17, 1994, that little deaf girl danced ballet to "Via Dolorosa" before a television audience of forty million . . . and was crowned Miss America. She had faith in her dream . . . and in her God.

I was that little girl. And I want you to know that dreams do come true. If they didn't, why would God design our hearts with the capacity to yearn for something greater than ourselves?

A dream is a journey, and though I may not know you personally, I know that God has a purpose and plan for your life . . . a dream for you. I believe God has a dream for each of us, and our greatest challenge and joy lies in finding and following that dream wherever it may lead. I'm only twenty-four years old, and I'm still on the journey, still following the dreams God has planned for me. Along the way I've become deaf, learned to talk, won the Miss America Pageant, traveled across America, married a wonderful man . . . and I'm still dreaming. I'm still listening to my heart. And I'd like you to know the joy of listening to your own heart and following your own dreams.

Before you can begin, you must believe that the journey to fulfill your dreams is possible. Someone once said that there is very little difference between one person and another, but what little there is is very important. The difference is *attitude*, and yours can be positive or negative, hopeful or hopeless. If you will believe that God cares and that he can lead you to fulfill his dreams for you, then you will find success.

We're not very different, you and I. By the time you've finished this book, I'm sure you'll know that I'm very human and far from perfect. But I've been amazed to learn that God can use anyone—even me—to influence the lives of others.

Why don't I tell you how my journey started?

The Revelation

In September 1974, my parents, Bill and Daphne Whitestone of Dothan, Alabama, were the parents of three girls: Stacey, four and a half; Melissa, three and a half; and me, eighteen months. September fourteenth began like any other day, but our lives were about to be changed forever. I awakened that morning with a slight fever. I was a normal, rambunctious toddler, and my mother had seen Stacey and Melissa through all kinds of childhood illnesses. My fever didn't worry her—at first.

But my fever climbed as the morning wore on, and by noontime it was so high that I had to be taken to the hospital. Even today the doctors and my parents aren't exactly sure what made me sick. But I was seriously ill, my fever soaring above 104 degrees. This was truly a life-or-death situation; and though I would ultimately survive, it was a defining event that would forever change my life and the way that I and my family lived.

In an effort to bring the fever down, my doctors gave me two different antibiotics which were both strong but risky. But extreme measures were necessary since I was close to death and the doctors knew these medicines could save my life. Unfortunately, there was also the possibility that I might suffer blindness, deafness, or mental retardation as side effects.

The antibiotics did work, though, and my fever subsided. After two weeks in the hospital, when the doctors were sure I was getting better, my parents took me home. But my recovery was not complete, and the massive infection I'd suffered left my body weak. I literally had to learn to walk and communicate again.

Two years ago, when I was home at Christmas, I watched a tape of Barbara Walters's interview with me and my mother. The interview included footage of me as a baby right after I had been released from the hospital. I had never seen this video clip, and I was so shocked at what I saw that my eyes welled with tears. I could not feed myself, I could not run with my sisters the way I had before my illness. I was just sitting almost motionless on the grass, supported by my young aunt Stephanie while my sisters rolled around on the grass.

That little girl, I thought, watching the image of myself, *looks as though she has no soul in her body. I can't believe that was me.*

There are no words that will adequately express my gratitude to my relatives who helped me recover from who I was at that time. For a long time they endured so many emotions and spent endless hours taking care of me. My physical therapy required that they exercise my body, brush my teeth, and feed me. I know it wasn't easy. Not only was my life changed, but my experience dramatically changed their lifestyle also. And while they worked with me, I'm sure they wondered if their efforts would have any effect—if I would ever be the same little girl they used to know.

On Christmas Day in 1974, circumstances proved that I was forever different. As my mother hurried about preparing the traditional holiday dinner for our extended family, she opened a kitchen cabinet and spilled a stack of pots and pans. The noise was so loud that everyone in the living room was startled. My grandmother, who with my aunt Stephanie had been watching me play by the Christmas tree, anxiously called Mother into the living room.

"Daphne," she said, nervously watching me. "I think there's something wrong with Heather's hearing. Stephanie and I nearly jumped out of our skins when you dropped those pans, but Heather didn't even look up."

Oblivious of the alarm in Grandmother's voice, I continued to play while Mom rushed back into the kitchen to grab a pan and a wooden spoon. The pretty lights of the Christmas tree and the colorful wrapping paper held my attention, as did the shiny new toys scattered over the floor.

Behind me, worlds away, my mother drowned out the Christmas carols on the stereo with her frantic banging and clanging.

I had no idea she was there.

Not yet being a parent myself, I can only imagine how parents of deaf children must feel at that moment of revelation. At least ninety percent of deaf children are born to hearing parents who have no prior experience with deafness. In my travels across America and in other countries, I have heard stories of heartbreak from parents who wonder why God has brought the tragedy and silence of deafness to their beloved child.

Let me assure you of this: Most very young deaf children have no reason to be *unhappy*. As a child, I didn't think of myself as deaf, I just thought of myself as "Heather." I didn't know what hearing was and couldn't remember my life before the fever, so I didn't know what I was missing. Like other children, I had joy and dreams in my heart. I truly believe that the most difficult and sad experience for deaf children is when they see their parents suffering and struggling.

Deafness isn't misery. I love the quote I heard one time: "Kindness is a language which the deaf can hear and the blind can see." Like any other child, I responded to and was warmed by my family's loving kindness.

After a series of tests, the doctors told my parents that I was profoundly deaf. They predicted that I would not develop much verbal speech. They told my parents to expect me not to develop beyond a third-grade education and recommended that some sort of vocational training be considered for me.

I am grateful that my parents did not accept the doctors' judgments without question. Out of their love they believed that much more was possible; they expected me to fulfill my God-given potential. Like love itself, they never gave up, never lost faith. They were always hopeful, they endured with me through every circumstance. They demonstrated a positive attitude, and I learned from their example. Their positive outlook was absolutely contagious.

Not that everything was always rosy. I know my parents went through a great deal of stress and worry as they weighed options and considered what was best for me. By the time I had completely recovered from my illness, tests revealed that I had at least a 120-decibel hearing loss in my right ear, and a 90-decibel hearing loss in my left ear—and that's when I'm wearing my hearing aid. Without it I hear nothing from either ear.

One recent evening, as I was taking off my hearing aid to go to bed, my husband asked if I could hear my own voice without my hearing aid. I was amazed at the question! I'd never really thought about it, but I had to tell him that I couldn't. I can feel a slight vibration in my lips, nose, and throat when I speak, but I can't hear anything without my hearing aid.

As a growing young girl, my deafness was an ever-present source of frustration. The innocence of early childhood passed all too quickly. I had to work hard every afternoon, and sometimes I had to say a word twenty times until I pronounced it correctly. My sisters would play outside after dinner, and I wanted to join them, but I couldn't get up from my work until I had finished my speech exercises. I thought it wasn't fair. Because of the discipline my deafness required, I developed a strong will and an independent streak as wide as Texas.

More than anything, my parents wanted me to live and learn and grow in the "real" world, the hearing world. From Doreen Pollack, director of speech and hearing services at Porter Memorial Hospital in Denver, they heard about the auditory verbal program called *acoupedics*. This approach to deaf education teaches deaf children to use their residual hearing to speak. It allows deaf children to amplify their hearing ability so they can live in the hearing world and attend regular schools.

Convinced that acoupedics was the right approach for me, my parents enrolled me in speech therapy . . . and public school.

Though my mother and I worked many long hours learning the skills of speech and listening that most children take for granted, I don't remember feeling different until one afternoon in second grade. During a fire drill, we spilled out of the class-room onto the playground. I was in the middle of my auditory training—for this training, my teacher, Beth Walker, wore a microphone. The electronic signal traveled from a black re-ceiver I wore on my belt through a cord, then into my earpiece. Mrs. Walker had always been fairly discreet about my deafness in the classroom, and few of my classmates really knew that I was "different." But suddenly there we were on the playground, open to everyone's inspection. I could feel all the kids who had never seen my hearing aid staring at the long cord trailing from my ear to the black box at my waist.

I was embarrassed and extremely conscious of their scru-tiny. "They're staring," I whispered to my teacher.

"Oh, Heather," she said, trying to put me at ease, "they just think you're wearing a radio."

She was kind, but I knew it wasn't true. I was different, and I didn't want to be.

I think this feeling of difference made me grow up faster than other children my age because I was always compensating, working harder, striving just to keep up. In the years since I won the Miss America crown, I've met many deaf children, and their most common question to me is "Do people treat you differently than they treat others?" Their eyes, so earnest and hopeful, look toward me for an answer, and I know I have to tell them the truth, that they do. When they know enough to ask that question, they have left the naïveté of childhood behind.

I tell them, "The world may treat you differently. People may not expect much of you. But you must not give up, you must follow your dreams. And you know what? You have already developed strong leadership because you choose to face obstacles and master them. You are a star because you believe in yourself. As long as you believe that you can follow your dreams, those who doubt you will gradually change their minds."

The Hiding Place

I was fortunate, though; I found a place of escape, a refuge from my feelings of being an outsider. The one place I felt accepted and "just like everyone else" was, strangely enough, in the dance studio. Hoping to improve the rhythm of my speech, my mother had enrolled me in a ballet class when I was five years old. There were only four dance studios in Dothan, and two were not willing to accept a deaf child. The Dothan School of Dance, however, accepted me.

Once, while I was visiting a community as Miss America, I was told about a dance teacher who would not allow two deaf girls to enroll in her dance class. These two little girls had seen my ballet performance on television and fell in love with ballet. When I heard that this teacher had denied them the opportunity to follow their dreams, I could imagine those two little girls crying in their bedrooms, their self-esteem destroyed. I would have loved to meet that dance teacher so I could explain that the most handicapped people on earth are those who are handicapped by negative thoughts and low expectations.

From the very moment I walked through the dance studio doorway, I loved everything about dancing! I loved wearing my pink tights and a leotard, I loved watching other dancers. They communicated with body language; words weren't necessary. I joined them, followed their movements, and was grateful that for once I didn't have to talk to make my feelings known. I also loved competing against them. I was determined to be the best, and really did not want the hearing students to dance better than me.

Because I was struggling with speech and frustrated with learning, ballet taught me a valuable lesson: patience. At the Dothan School of Dance, my instructor, Patti Rutland, taught me that I'd have to be patient and wait for my muscles to develop, I'd have to be patient to hear and learn the music, I'd have to be patient and wait until the other students had finished their dance. In ballet I learned to respect the learning process.

And dancing began to fill my dreams. It became the place where my thoughts could soar. In every free moment I dreamed of twirling in the spotlight. At night I left my hearing aid on and went to bed listening to classical music so I could dream of dancing. Dancing was my escape from the difficulty and frustration of learning. As I leapt and jumped and twirled, I could leave the trials of communication behind.

Not that life was totally frustrating. I loved playing with Melissa, my sister. We were the best of friends. We rode bikes together, explored the woods in our neighborhood, swam, and played games. Melissa and I shared a great love for animals. Since our family didn't have any pets, we frequently "adopted" the neighbors': We'd bring their cats to our home and feed them bowls of milk. Often we would dress up our stuffed animals and take them up and down the street in our little wagon. We'd put each stuffed animal in one of the neighbor's mailboxes. Once we had "delivered" all the animals, we'd pretend we were bus drivers and our wagon the school bus. We'd go back to the mailboxes and pick up our "passengers."

When Melissa wasn't around, I played in a little garden I had established in our backyard. Since we never had a pet, I enjoyed lavishing care and attention on plants. I've always had a love for nature, and I felt close to God when I was outside with my hands in the soil.

I'm not the only one to feel close to God through nature. In her book, *A Gift for God*, Mother Teresa says that God "cannot be found in noise and restlessness. God is the friend of silence. See how nature—trees, flowers, grass—grows in silence; see the stars, the moon and the sun, how they move in silence. . . . We need silence to be able to touch souls."

Nature was my friend; I enjoyed its silence. I recently read that deaf children often form a special bond with animals because animals communicate without words. Since we had no pets, plants were like pets to me, and I learned that each different variety of plant had to be treated differently—some liked the sun, others preferred the shade. I learned how to tell when they were thirsty and when they needed fertilizer. Sometimes I felt as if my plants were babies who couldn't communicate, but needed someone to look after them.

As a child gardener, I somehow sensed that God gave nature to us as a gift. By taking care of nature, I felt I was honoring God himself. God took care of me, so I wanted to serve him by taking care of his creation.

Every weekend my father took my sisters and me to Panama City Beach. There we'd play in the surf or ride on his boat. It was a wonderful time of relaxation, and I listened to God's voice as I stared at the wide expanse of rolling gulf and enjoyed the sun. Often we slept on Dad's sailboat.

Once on the boat I remember Melissa waking me at two o'clock in the morning. She was frustrated because Dad's snoring was keeping her awake while I was sleeping peacefully! I was mad that she woke me. "What are you doing?" I snapped at her.

"I can't sleep because Dad is snoring. But you were sleeping like an angel."

Curious, I turned my hearing aid on to listen. Goodness, but Dad was loud, and he sounded something like a pig! I was glad then that I was deaf. "Too bad, Melissa," I said, turning my hearing aid off again. I rolled over and settled down to sleep. "But you've got to be deaf to get any sleep around here."

When I wasn't dancing, gardening, or doing homework, I was daydreaming. I still enjoy using my imagination, since it is there that I can get away from the world, gather my thoughts, and envision the future. Don't think that daydreaming is a completely frivolous activity. Long before 1994, I'd stand in the bathroom before the mirror with a headband on my head and pretend I was Miss America! While my sisters were beating on the door to get in the bathroom, I was pretending to answer questions from reporters and other curious people. I'm sure they didn't think all that practice was ever going to be terribly useful.

At other times I would bother my sisters by doing my ballet jumps in front of the TV while they were watching it. Melissa and Stacey would get mad. "Get out of the way," they'd yell. "Who do you think you are, Miss America?"

For all our normal, ordinary squabbling, I was very lucky to have two sisters who treated me like any normal sister and not like a deaf kid. They looked at me as a person, not as a handicapped person. Stacey treated me like any girl treats her nosy little sister, and Melissa was my best friend. My sisters (who are both married now with wonderful families of their own) added color and richness to my life. Nearly all of my childhood relationships were ordinary and normal.

All but one. My mother and I were different from other mothers and daughters. As a child, I noticed the difference and was puzzled by it. Now I understand and am grateful for all my mother did for me—she taught me to sew, took me on vacations, and introduced me to music—but in my youth I couldn't understand why Mother and I seemed to do nothing but work together.

After dinner, while Stacey and Melissa had to wash dishes, Mother and I settled down to tackle my schoolwork. Stacey and Melissa didn't think it was fair, but they didn't know there were many times I'd have given anything to put away the books and join them at the sink!

Schoolwork was difficult and extremely time-consuming. I was a slow reader, and had to especially concentrate on English grammar. To this day, I don't like to write; it's difficult to read and write a language you never really hear. Learning seemed to take forever, and in school I had to concentrate twice as hard as the other students. Because I couldn't take notes and read lips at the same time, I had to tape-record the teacher's lesson, then have a family member play the tape back and take notes for me. Only then could I study the notes for myself. I was often tired and suffered from headaches related to the stress and pressure. Sometimes I think I spent most of my childhood doing homework.

I often felt sorry for my mother. After helping me with my homework, she'd have to stay up late at night to finish her own work. She taught middle school during my elementary years, and she'd be up late grading papers and planning lessons. In the morning she'd come into the kitchen with dark shadows and lines of weariness around her eyes.

On those early mornings, looking at my mom, I wished as much for her as for myself that I wasn't deaf.

But though I worked hard, I'll be the first to tell you I'm not a saint. I often became frustrated, even angry. I was eager to learn, but my deafness slowed me down. It was as if I were wading through thick mud while everyone else scampered ahead of me on dry ground. I knew I was smart, I could memorize easily, but I worked until I was exhausted and seemed to make little headway despite my efforts.

I did get depressed. At school I'd eat lunch every day in a sea of rollicking children who laughed and talked and smiled and pointed while I didn't have the faintest idea why they were laughing, smiling, and pointing. I withdrew into my daydreams, often imagining myself dancing in a bright spotlight.

A Glimpse of the Deaf World

Beth Walker, my speech teacher in elementary school, gave me a book about a deaf dancer who went to a special school for the deaf and spoke sign language. I also read a book about Helen Keller—the story of Helen Keller was required reading for everyone in my class. Reading these women's stories, I realized for the first time that there were other deaf people in the world, and I wanted to meet them. I also became curious about sign language. My parents had not allowed me to use sign language at home since they wanted to make sure I was able to communicate with everyone. Even though I learned to sign before I was five when I was in a class with signing deaf students, by the time I was eleven I had forgotten all the sign language I had learned.

I understand now why my parents did not allow me to sign at home, and I'm grateful that I can communicate with anyone at any time—I don't have to wait for a sign language interpreter to show up and become my voice. I can walk into any McDonald's and order a hamburger and soft drink for myself.

I use my speaking ability much more often than sign language. Sign language is relatively easy to learn; however, learning to speak is not easy. It is the most difficult—for parent and child—the most expensive, and the most time-consuming option. I still have to visit a speech therapist once in a while. It's like exercise. In order to stay in shape, you have to continue to work out.

By the time I was eleven and in the fourth grade, I knew I was falling behind in my English language skills and I wanted to catch up with my classmates. I desperately wanted to go to a school for the deaf, and couldn't understand why my parents didn't immediately agree to send me. Of course, I had no idea that such schools cost a great deal of money. I also couldn't understand all the difficult emotions involved when parents choose to send a young child to a boarding school far away from home. Though an easy enough issue for me, for my parents this would not be an easy decision.

This was a pivotal time for me. Up until this point I'd worked and played within the safe confines of my sheltering family, but as all children do, I began to turn my gaze outward. I looked around at my classmates, then I looked at myself. I wore a hearing aid; no one else did. I had to make tremendous effort learning how to communicate while it came naturally to others around me. Most of the other kids had lots of friends, I had only my sisters and Claudia, a friend from my neighborhood. Everyone else around me seemed to know where they fit in. But for me there wasn't anyone who shared my experiences, and it was difficult to build my identity without others who shared some of my circumstances. I was deaf; no one else was.

My answer? A school for the deaf. At such a school I could learn how to take my own notes and become an independent student. My family could have normal lives. And I could finally find others like me.

My parents also came to see this as the best decision for my future, despite their worries about it. After checking out several schools, my parents enrolled me at the Central Institute for the Deaf in St. Louis, Missouri. Dr. Jean Moog, the principal at that time, ran an excellent program.

Dr. Moog and her teachers believed in reading lips as opposed to signing only. The program there also emphasized strong writing skills. Among other things, they taught me how to take my own notes, how to understand the structure of a paragraph, and how to study. I was eleven years old when I entered CID and was reading at a second grade level. I pushed myself hard during my three years there and was able to make up the years I was behind, advancing two grade levels per year.

CID is unique not only because it is designed for deaf students, but because it is an international school. My roommate, Grace Lee, was a Canadian of Korean descent. One boy, Fadi (whom I thought was kind of cute and whom I must admit I had a crush on), was from Kuwait. I became good friends with Blanca from Chicago, who was Latino, and Bola, who came from northern Africa. Though we had come to CID from different places, I never saw my classmates as different types of people because we had the same heart and the same mind. We were all simply trying our best to be successful and we all struggled against similar obstacles. Each of my classmates told me stories and shared insights I could never have picked up living in a small town in Alabama. I was excited to be in St. Louis, a big city, and I couldn't wait to discover the new worlds that seemed to be opening before me.

I lived with other CID students in a dorm located in downtown St. Louis. Our classes were small, with three or four students per teacher, and we were encouraged in all ways to be as independent as possible. After school we would typically visit the St. Louis museums or zoos, or participate in sports or dance classes. There were no ballet lessons available during the years I was at CID, and though I missed ballet very much, I knew my time at CID was important.

One person at CID who had a tremendous influence on my life was Jim Marco. Mr. Marco, the physical education coach, introduced me to soccer, baseball, track and field, volleyball, floor hockey, ice skating, basketball, and orienteering. Being away from my family, I missed strong central adults in my life and came to look upon him as a father figure. He was a terrific support to me and was always fostering the independent spirit that was so important at CID. He believed that deaf students could compete against hearing people. He had faith in us, and he cared enough to teach us even about things that had nothing to do with sports.

I remember one afternoon when my friends and I were fighting—a typical girls' argument. Mr. Marco, who heard us as he was walking by, stopped and made us all sit down at a table in the dorm. "Let me tell you about life," he said, fixing us in a no-nonsense gaze. "I've learned the hard way that fighting is a waste of time and energy. Life is time, and it's ridiculous to waste your life this way."

Even though he taught us many lessons like this, he didn't talk down to us. He talked to us as if we were mature and not just a group of silly twelve-year-olds. He believed in us, and because he did, we began to believe in ourselves. And he was right about how we should spend our lives. Someone once said, "Life is a coin. You can spend it any way you wish, but you can spend it only once." Mr. Marco really made this clear to his students, and he showed me that life is precious and not to be wasted.

One of my fondest memories of Mr. Marco was learning the sport of orienteering from him—a popular competition that involves being dropped off in unfamiliar woods with a map and a compass. The athlete has to find his or her way through a series of checkpoints to a finish line some distance away as quickly as he or she can.

I loved orienteering because I loved being in the woods. The woods were so peaceful! In a sense I was used to being away from other people, so the silence of the woods didn't bother me, and I never felt alone because the woods are like a cathedral; God's presence is so strong. There were many moments when I had a real sense of serenity and of wonder, such as when a red fox ran by a few feet away, stunning me with his beauty.

Believe it or not, I never really got lost while orienteering. There were times when I wandered around a bit, but I always found my way back and no one ever had to look for me. Though I know it wasn't exactly the right attitude, I was secretly a little proud when others got lost and had to be rescued by the adults. I was proud and excited to have found something I was good at despite my age, despite my deafness. I reveled in my feelings of self-sufficiency, discovering that I really could take care of myself.

I began to enter orienteering competitions because orienteering increased my self-esteem, and I found that I also loved the thrill of competition. Competing on an equal footing with hearing people assured me that my mind and heart were no different from theirs, and when I won the state orienteering championship, my self-confidence increased by leaps and bounds. I'm sure that God used this competition to help me on the journey toward my dream because by the time I began to compete in pageants, I was already used to intense competitive experiences. I was not nearly as nervous as I would have been without these adventures.

One of the best things about going to school in St. Louis was my priceless friendship with Grace Lee, my roommate. Grace was a year younger than me, but she was so intelligent and clever that she constantly motivated me to achieve. We studied together and fought like sisters, but we forgave each other easily. We called each other "bosom friends" because we were as close as Anne and Diana in *Anne of Green Gables*. One day we went to the park in front of the school and made chains of flowers, wove them into wreaths, then wore them as crowns to symbolize our friendship. We comforted and encouraged each other as we galvanized each other to keep achieving. We were constantly asking, "Who's smarter? Me or you?" Though I knew Grace was a lot smarter than me, we competed to see who could get the highest grades and do the best work. We were both very determined not to use our deafness as an excuse, but to strive for our dreams. Grace was an exceptionally talented artist, and I imagined her becoming a famous fashion designer. I had to find some dream equally as grand as the one I'd conjured for her, so now I not only dreamed of being a ballerina, I imagined myself as a *famous* ballerina. Something magic happened between us, and we brought out the best in each other.

Even when we were working hard we could always make each other laugh. I'll never forget one afternoon in math class when our teacher excused himself and stepped out of the room. We were in auditory training and were wearing what we called the "phonic ear"—the earpiece and receiver that transmitted the teacher's amplified voice from his microphone to our hearing aids. After our teacher left the room still wearing his microphone, Grace looked up at me. "What's that sound?" she asked, crinkling her nose. "It sounds like rain." She looked up at the windows, confused, because outside the sun was shining and the sky was blue.

I bit my lip, stifling the urge to laugh. My hearing was a little better than Grace's, and I'd heard the teacher's footsteps as he walked into the rest room. The loud flushing sound in our ears a moment later erased Grace's confusion, and we dissolved into giggles. We were still laughing when our teacher returned and we told him he had forgotten to turn off his microphone.

I have so many good memories of CID—even the bad memories are fun to revisit now. On my thirteenth birthday I remember waking up and feeling sick. I'd come down with the flu, and spent the rest of the day groaning on a bed in the nurse's room while Grace and my friends enjoyed my birthday cake!

And once Bola told me a story I'll never forget—she said one night she'd seen a beautiful angel in her bedroom. The idea of seeing an angel didn't frighten me at all. I had grown up in the Episcopal church and knew about God, even though I couldn't follow the service and found the King James Bible hard to read and understand. So while the pastor talked, I made music in my heart and daydreamed about dancing to God's glory in the church. Sometimes at home, alone in the living room, I danced for God, just for his pleasure.

And every night as I lay in bed in the dorm at CID, I'd dream about dancing and watch for the angels Bola had spoken of, hoping to see one before I fell asleep. I believed God loved me, and I wouldn't have been at all surprised to see a heavenly guardian watching over us in the dorm.

At fourteen I was ready for graduation from CID. I can honestly say that I owe much of my success to that school and Dr. Moog. Without the lessons I learned there, I doubt I could have succeeded in high school, much less have continued on to college. I certainly wouldn't have become Miss America, because the pageant requires good grades! CID was the beginning of my academic journey . . . the commencement of a dream fulfilled.

Now that I had learned so much, I was not afraid to go back to Dothan and enter public high school, but I hated having to say good-bye to the many friends I'd made in St. Louis. Leaving was especially difficult because I had learned so much about myself. I knew that I was not the same little girl I had been when I left Dothan, and I was afraid that my friends in Alabama had grown up and moved on too.

The summer after my graduation, my family and I went to Panama City Beach for a vacation. It felt good to rest, because I was mentally bracing myself for high school. I'd be the only deaf student at my public school, Northview High, and I knew that there would be many challenges for me.

Returning to Public School

Once we returned from Panama City, I learned that my fears about my old friends moving on were not unfounded. Claudia, my best friend before I went to St. Louis, was now in eighth grade, a cheerleader, and a completely different person from the little girl I'd known. I didn't blame her, of course, for changing, because I had changed too. I was also supposed to be in eighth grade, but had advanced far enough at CID that I could enroll in ninth grade on my return. When school began, I trudged through the halls alone, surrounded by milling bodies and noise that I couldn't decipher. Lunchtime seemed woven of eternity; I thought it would never end. Seeing everyone laughing and talking together while I sat alone made me miss my days in St. Louis when I was also part of the crowd. In class I took notes as I read the textbooks because I noticed that the teachers often repeated the same material that was in the text. I remember thinking that my teachers—and fellow students— seemed a lot less serious than the people I'd known at CID. My fellow students seemed to care more about after-school activities and football games and cars than they did about their studies.

In comparison to the strict discipline at CID, the students at Northview High School seemed wild. Not all of them were, of course, but for the first time I saw students smoking and drinking openly.

There were also racial problems at Northview. I couldn't believe how dangerous my school was. Sometimes huge fights would break out because of people's racial prejudice, and as many as fifty police officers would be dispatched to the school. For me, school was for learning, not fighting, and at CID I had learned to be friendly with people from all over the world, from many different backgrounds. The color of a person's skin didn't matter to me, so it really bewildered me when students of different racial backgrounds couldn't get along.

But this was what the world was like, and in Dothan I learned to deal with reality. For the first time in my sheltered life I realized that dangers are not confined to places "out there" and that you can be in danger no matter where you are.

Very few students at Northview took the time to communicate with me, and that made my time there difficult. But I resumed my ballet classes, and the dance studio once again became my safe haven. As I danced more and more, the dreams I'd had in my CID dorm sharpened and came into focus—why *couldn't* I become a professional ballerina? I decided to pursue that goal with my whole heart. Life as a dancer seemed a beautiful and peaceful existence, an escape from the rough and dangerous real world.

There were people who thought I would never succeed, but I was determined to listen to my heart's positive attitude, not to other people's low expectations. After all, dancers had heads, arms, feet, and hearts—everything I had. I dance to music coming from my heart, not my ears, and in the beginning I just had to work extra hard to move the music from my hearing aid into my heart.

Ralph Lauren once told the *International Herald Tribune*, "People ask how can a Jewish kid from the Bronx do preppy clothes? Does it have to do with class and money? It has to do with dreams."

Becoming a ballerina was my dream, and I was determined not to let anybody take it away. Young life is like a blank page, full of opportunity, but sadly, too many children will take adults as the final voice in everything and do not have confidence in their own aspirations. When they are told they can't do something, they won't try to do it. But we all have a right to dream.

But our dreams have to be realistic if we're to live in the real world. There were days when I wondered if I would ever get a job, have a family of my own, and lead an independent life. I'd spent years learning to be independent; I certainly didn't want to depend upon my family for the rest of my days. I wanted to be a successful professional ballerina, yet I worried about what kind of life awaited me. The time demands of school, though, prevented me from having the opportunity to gain real-world work experience. And I was deaf. Why would anyone hire a deaf person with no experience?

When I had dark thoughts like these, I was overcome with feelings of despair about my future and the burden I had already been to my family. I wanted desperately to succeed in whatever I did, because only then would I truly be independent . . . and it was the only way my family would be free of caring for and worrying about me.

Though I would have given anything to forget about school and dance with a ballet company, I knew an education was terribly important. I would still pursue my dream, but I wanted it to be realistic, and it was clear I needed as much education as I could get. My parents reinforced the importance of education and kept pushing me toward college, but I would still get frustrated that I didn't have more time for dance. Truly great ballerinas enter a ballet company in their mid-teens. I was told that dancing could wait, but it couldn't, not really. A dancer's prime is a fleeting thing, and young dancers must begin early and train hard. How could I do both?

Yet even though I couldn't see how I possibly could have both education and my dream, I clung even more tightly to my vision of dancing—before millions. I would make a difference . . . somehow. And since God had given me the dream of dancing, I had faith that he would make a way for it to come true.

Troubled Times

I used dance not only as an escape from school, but also as an escape from home. My school environment was not the only thing that had changed when I came back from CID. Home, too, was entirely different. For the first time, I felt lonely in my own house. Melissa, my sister and my best friend, and I had grown apart.

Melissa, like Stacey, was very involved in youth government. The year I was away in St. Louis, Stacey had been elected youth governor for the state of Alabama. That accomplishment really astounded me, and I remember thinking, "Why, Stacey is an ordinary person! If my sister can become youth governor, success can happen to *anybody!*"

In that moment I realized that you don't have to be born rich or famous or *hearing* to realize your dreams. So in high school I followed my sisters into youth government, but soon grew to dislike it. The activities revolved around conversation, and since I missed most of the dialogue that went on around me, after a while I lost interest.

The house seemed empty and quiet. Melissa continued her quest to follow in Stacey's footsteps. Stacey had left home for the Air Force Academy, and when Melissa wasn't working on her school activities, she was dating. I missed Grace terribly, and was keenly disappointed that Melissa was not the doting sister she had been before I left. Mother was busy with her schoolwork, Dad spent hours in front of the television watching the news. I retreated to my room and began to read the Bible.

My sisters and I were raised in the church. But when we went to Sunday school and the weekly worship service, I couldn't understand a word that was said. So though I knew God was real and he loved me, I suppose you could say I didn't have a very strong impression of who he was.

To me, in those days, God was sort of like the wind I felt at the beach. I could feel his power, I saw the effects of his strength, and I was comforted by his closeness, just as I enjoyed the ocean breezes on my face. But I had never given much thought to the possibility that he might personally care for me.

During those quiet hours at home I began to want to know more about God. The more I learned about Jesus, the more I wanted to learn about him. So I began to study his word. I thought I could please God by being a good girl and doing good things. I thought if I was good enough, God would accept me. I tried to follow his commandments . . . and found that task a lot harder than I expected.

Meanwhile, outside my bedroom, Mom and Dad were fighting a lot. I was surprised to hear from Melissa that they'd been fighting for a long time. Of course I'd missed all the family turmoil while I was away in St. Louis, and now when they fought I couldn't hear a word of their argument. I remember once going into Melissa's bedroom when Mom and Dad began to argue. Melissa turned up the volume on her radio so she couldn't hear their fight. I begged her to tell me what they were arguing about, but she wouldn't say—in fact, she said she'd stopped paying attention long ago. They had always argued, she said, but things had lately grown worse.

I suppose my deafness was a hidden blessing because I didn't have to listen to my parents' arguments. I wanted to know what was going on, but no one would tell me.

One day the seriousness of their conflict became all too clear. I was surprised to see that Mom had arrived home from school before we did, and when I walked through the front door I noticed that some of our furniture was missing. I was shocked. During my years at CID, some of my friends asked if my parents were divorced, and I was always proud to say, "No, my parents are together." Now I was just like my friends—a child of divorce. Never again would my parents live together.

Like all children in similar situations, divorce changed my life forever. Mom and Dad had experienced troubles in the past, but they had always managed to pull things together. This time when I told Dad that he had to work things out, he said, "Trust me, Heather, it's too hard. It's too painful. It's hopeless. We're not going to make it." Mom said the same thing too. But deep in my heart I thought they could overcome their difficulties if they tried.

I remember praying a lot about their breakup. I actually went as far as to tell my mother that God doesn't like divorce, and she turned away, not pleased with the idea of her daughter preaching to her. That's when I realized that I could not control other people's feelings and saw that my dream of a reconciliation between my parents would not come true. But though I ached inside, God spoke to my heart and comforted me just like he comforts everyone who turns to him when a cherished dream vanishes like breath upon a mirror.

Perhaps the most painful thing about my parents' divorce was that I—like almost all children of divorced parents—felt forced to choose sides. Before the divorce, I never had to censor myself and talk about only half the family. After the divorce, I had to decide who to visit during holidays, feeling that I would upset whichever parent I didn't choose. Holidays used to be wonderful, now they are complicated and guilt-inducing.

Soon after my parents' divorce, my mother decided to move

back to her hometown of Birmingham, where her family still lived. She reassumed her maiden name, Daphne Gray, and uprooted us for the move. I must admit that I was excited about the opportunities of a larger city. I knew the Alabama School of Fine Arts was located in Birmingham, and that it was a public school, not expensive like the private arts schools where I'd been hoping to go. Sonia Arova, the dance teacher there, was a ballerina who had danced with Rudolf Nureyev. She allowed me to enroll without the required audition because she said she had seen me dance at a summer dance camp and thought I did a wonderful job. I was thrilled!

The Alabama School of Fine Arts

Gaining admission into the Alabama School of Fine Arts felt like winning a gold medal. Mother was concerned because the school was located downtown in a high crime area, but I was so intent upon becoming a ballerina that she relented. I was happy that the teachers there looked past my disability and saw my positive attitude. I felt really accepted there.

The Alabama School of Fine Arts was all I'd hoped it would be—and less. It was a small school with lots of art and no cheerleaders or football team. The ballet program was wonderful, and I was thrilled to be dancing three or four hours a day. In my regular public school classes, I dreamed of ballet when I was supposed to be paying attention. I didn't have to daydream at the Alabama School of Fine Arts because I was too busy dancing!

But the academics proved difficult for me. The classroom walls were insubstantial structures that didn't reach to the ceiling, and noise floated over the top and made it difficult for me to hear the teacher. I don't know if you've ever had an opportunity to hear through a hearing aid, but a mechanical ear doesn't discriminate. It picks up and amplifies every sound, much like a tape recorder indiscriminately picks up every bird chirp and passing car when you're recording something out of doors. Keeping up with my academic work was a struggle. My mother and Aunt Stephanie and I had to work hard to complete my schoolwork, and after a few months we were all exhausted.

Christmas break provided a welcome change in more ways than one. One of the highlights of my year came when students from the Alabama School of Fine Arts were selected to dance in the annual production of *The Nutcracker* performed by the Alabama Ballet Company. I danced that year as a candy cane, and though I was thrilled to be part of the ABC production, my heart writhed in disappointment because I hadn't been chosen for a more substantial part. I wanted to be Clara or one of the little girls dancing at the Christmas party. The candy cane part was easy, anybody could have danced it. Some part of me wondered for an instant if they hadn't chosen me for a bigger role because of my deafness, but I quickly put that thought away. It does no good to dwell on negative thoughts.

I shouldered my disappointment and tried to concentrate on the positive aspects of being in the production. Sure, the candy cane was a small, easy part, but it got me backstage! I had a free ticket to watch professional ballerinas every night, so I sat on the floor backstage and studied the dancers warming up. It was a wonderful experience.

But the relaxed spirit of Christmas passed all too quickly, and soon the charm of the School of Fine Arts wore off. I finished out the year, but the strenuous academic work was taking a toll on my mother, my relatives, and me. Because of this, I transferred the following year to Berry High School and began to dance at the Briarwood Presbyterian Church.

Barbara Barker founded the Briarwood Ballet as a Christian

dance company dedicated to teaching and performing dance as a form of worship. When I danced with the other dancers from Briarwood, I saw that they understood what I'd felt all my life: Dancing is a natural, expressive way to bring praise and glory to God.

I had first come to this conclusion one Christmas Eve when I was very young. I waited until everyone in the house went to bed, then I slipped into the living room and turned on the Christmas-tree lights. Caught by the wonder and spirit of Christmas, I pretended to be the Virgin Mary. With a baby doll we used to represent the infant Jesus, I danced around the tree, offering my dance as a celebratory gift to God. It became my secret, personal tradition which I repeated every year, and I always felt that God enjoyed it tremendously.

I loved dancing at Briarwood, but school at Berry High was as lonely as it had been at Northview. I was so quiet and shy that only a few students took the time to get to know me, so I invested my time and energy in schoolwork and dance. But even in the dance studio I had become sort of a misfit. I felt I was the oldest girl in the class—an eleventh grader amid younger high school and junior high school girls—because most girls my age had "graduated" to other, more "grown-up" activities like dating and cheerleading.

My loneliness was eased, though, because at that time I discovered what it meant to have a *personal* relationship with Jesus Christ. I had heard about Jesus ever since I was little, but I never understood that I needed to make a decision to ask Jesus to be my savior. In my efforts to please God and be good, I had joined a youth group at Shades Mountain Baptist Church, and one Sunday the teacher asked me if I had been baptized. I told her that I had been baptized as a baby in the Episcopal church, and I thought I was "saved" all my life. But even though I loved Jesus and had talked about him since childhood, I did not read the Bible or pray consistently until this point in my life, when I literally surrendered my life to him. I had believed that he existed, I had believed in his goodness and love. Finally, I was ready to *believe* in him enough to trust my life and my future to him.

I learned that just being good wouldn't cut it with God. Besides, I knew my own failings, and there was no way I could ever be good enough to please a perfect, holy God. I had to stop counting on my efforts at goodness and trust in *Jesus'* efforts to reach me.

I needed a supernatural friend by my side in high school. Although I was somewhat close to one girl who took a sign language class with me, I had very few real friends at Berry. As before, I found myself sitting in the cafeteria with kids who seemed to have known one another since kindergarten. I tried to read their lips, but since they all talked at the same time, I caught very little of the conversation. I had to constantly ask, "What did she say?" and assumed my classmates would grow tired of having to continually repeat themselves for me. After a while I gave up and just laughed when they laughed and smiled when they smiled, though I didn't have a clue as to what was going on. While they talked about their dates, hobbies, games, clubs, activities, and whatever else kids talk about, my mind was filled with dreams of spotlights and toe shoes.

This habit of withdrawal is one I've never shed. I suppose this tendency to quietly fall back is the result of my constant yearning to fit in. Anyone who has ever been left out of a playground game or a lunchroom conversation knows the strength of the human desire to participate. As a deaf person, the struggle to fit in is lifelong.

Once, sitting in the classroom at Berry, I remember being

smitten with jealousy as I watched one of the popular girls laughing with her friends. At that moment I would have given anything to have switched places with her, but I knew I couldn't. Even though I would have never wanted to give up my ballet, I always wanted to be a homecoming queen or a cheerleader—something that would have made me feel accepted by everyone and maybe even admired. It was very difficult for me to feel so left out of the life everyone else seemed to share. *One day*, I told myself, *I'll prove to them that I'm something. I will find something better than popularity, more outstanding than cheerleading . . .*

Sometimes I was angry. *Why don't they take the time to be my friend?* I'd wonder. *Why don't they talk to me? I have a brain, I can read lips, but someone's got to talk to me first!*

But even in my anger I didn't really feel *worthy* of their friendship. I longed for something to make me acceptable in their eyes. Then, during my senior year, I flipped through an old yearbook and noticed the section for senior superlatives: best dressed, most athletic, most popular, etc. In this section I saw the picture included each year of the Berry High girls who participated in the annual Junior Miss Pageant.

More than anything, I wanted to be a superlative *something*. I was nearing the end of my high school days and had been active in just one club, the Junior Civitan Club. But I wanted my yearbook "presence" to be more than a class picture people would point to in years to come and say, "Yeah, I remember her. The deaf girl."

Because I wanted to have something special to show to my children, I decided to enter my first pageant—the Shelby County Junior Miss program. Even though I didn't win—I was second runner-up—this was a great experience because it brought me out of my isolation and helped me relate to girls my own age.

Part of the pageant program involved a choreographed routine, and some of the girls were having difficulty with the dance steps. I was more than happy to help them out. I was thrilled to be useful, and I think they were surprised to find out that it was possible—even easy—to communicate with me. I took a lot of time to help them, and they followed my lead in the dance. Their gratitude lifted my self-esteem in a way I'd never experienced before. And on the final night of the pageant, when the emcee announced that I had won the "Spirit Award"—a scholarship awarded by the contestants themselves—I felt as happy as if I'd been voted homecoming queen of a dozen high schools.

After the pageant I floated home on a cloud of pure bliss. From my awards I had earned $1,400 toward my college expenses, plus I'd won the talent competition. It was wonderful to have such recognition for my dancing. My sagging self-esteem was now steadily on the rise. I also learned that God has his own way of praising his children. Being homecoming queen wasn't his plan for me. He had another plan.

A tiny flurry of publicity about me followed the Shelby County Junior Miss Pageant. Our school newspaper ran a small article, plus the local newspaper did a piece on the pageant and mentioned my talent along with the fact that I'd been second runner-up. But our school district included students from two counties—Shelby County and Jefferson County—so only one other girl from my school had been in my pageant. The vast majority of girls from my school had entered the Jefferson County Junior Miss pageant, so I hadn't had the chance to meet and befriend many of my classmates.

Though I had made a lot of new friends at the pageant, school was as lonely as it had always been. I did meet my goal—my picture would be in the high school yearbook as a Junior Miss contestant—but I had only a few friends. When my mother saw my long face during the weeks after the pageant, I assured her I wasn't upset at not winning. I was just lonely.

Though I had confidence in God's loving plan for my life, it wasn't always easy to wait quietly for it to unfold. Like all teenage girls, I fretted—sometimes a little, sometimes a lot— because the boys weren't exactly beating down our door to take me out. Like all girls, I suppose, I thought the guys weren't asking me out because I was ugly, fat, and dumb, though I knew down deep inside that no one wanted to date me because of my disability. It seemed that my fellow high school students only wanted to hang around kids who were perfect, and I certainly didn't fit *that* bill.

The Junior Miss Pageant, though, did bring an unexpected date my way. Nobody at Berry High ever asked me out—I don't know if they were afraid of my deafness or bewildered by my shyness, but after the Junior Miss Pageant and the resulting newspaper articles, I did get two dates with guys who were hearing-impaired. The first date was arranged by the young man's sister, and I colored with embarrassment when I learned I'd have to drive over and pick him up. I went because I didn't want to hurt his feelings, but the experience was a far cry from the romantic first date I'd dreamed of having. Where was the knight on the white horse to sweep me off my feet? I couldn't see him within a hundred miles of our house.

Another young man, a deaf football player from another school, read about me in one of the newspaper articles and asked me out. He was a nice young man, but he wasn't for me, and so we didn't go out more than once.

As my senior year rapidly drew to a close, I didn't have a date for the one event that really mattered—the senior prom. The previous year I had sat at home during Berry High's junior prom and was now determined not to miss my senior prom, because I wanted desperately to tell my children about that supposedly magical night. As the time drew near and nobody asked me to go, I went to my mother for advice. She advised me that sometimes the straightforward approach is best.

So I went to the school office and asked a secretary who was also a good friend of mine, "Do you know a good Christian guy I can ask to the prom?" She grinned and recommended a shy, auburn-haired senior named Dave Bush.

Later that day I found him in the hall and, with my heart in my throat, I carefully approached him. "David," I asked, watching his face for any hint that he might turn and run, "are you going to the prom?"

"No, I'm not," he answered a bit cautiously.

That was good. He hadn't run, and I hadn't fainted. "Me either," I went on, managing a nervous smile. "And I want to go to the prom with a friend. Would you like to come with me?"

Poor David's face reddened, and I was embarrassed for him. I thought I had put him in a difficult situation since he didn't want to go with me because of my deafness, but I realized later that he was just very shy. He took a deep breath and accepted my invitation. We smiled. I suggested that to save money we might skip dinner before the prom, but a few days later David asked me if I would go to dinner with him. I was pleasantly surprised, and accepted.

I was very excited about the prom, but there was one thing I wanted to talk about with David before the big night. Alone in my room that night, I wrote him a note:

> *David, there is something I want you to know. I have made the most important decision in my whole life, to accept Jesus Christ as my savior. I promised God that I would not do anything with my date that would displease him. I have dedicated my life and my body to God. I'm committed to wait until I have vowed my marriage vows.*

So I want my senior prom to be special without any trouble. I hope you understand how I feel. David, will you help me keep my promise to God on this prom date?

Before giving the note to David, I prayed that God would help him understand how important Jesus Christ was to me. When he received my note, David was completely supportive of my commitment.

My entire family helped me prepare for that special affair. My grandmother Whitestone and Aunt Gloria took me shopping for my prom dress, and I was thrilled because the sequined fuchsia dress was my first formal gown. The gown I had worn in the Shelby County Junior Miss Pageant was the bridesmaid's dress I had worn in my sister Stacey's wedding.

Our prom was a fun-filled evening. David was a complete gentleman on that date—in fact, he even suggested that we leave an after-prom party where the students were drinking— and I'll always be grateful to him for making my prom memories special.

In coaching me for this special evening, my aunt Stephanie had suggested that I give David a good-night kiss. "Just a kiss on the cheek to thank him for treating you with respect," she said, waving her hands in frustration because I kept insisting that I wouldn't kiss on the first date.

And so, at the conclusion of the evening, though I was so nervous my knees knocked, I leaned forward and gave him a tiny kiss on the cheek. David turned as red as a rose—and I beat a hasty retreat inside the house.

My husband, John, loves teasing me about that story—I made him wait six months before I would kiss him, and then he got only a kiss on the cheek too! But, as I've told him, I had to make sure it was *me* he liked, and not Miss America!

My senior prom came and went in May 1991. As soon as

my excitement over the prom subsided, I began to concentrate again on my dancing. The Miss Deaf Alabama Pageant was scheduled for June, and I had to rehearse and plan and practice.

I had begun to realize that pageants were a way to make friends *and* earn scholarship money. Pageants, I thought, just might be a way to make my dreams come true.

2 The Road to Atlantic City

Journal entry,
November 29, 1989:

With God, everything is possible. Tonight I watched a
movie called *Prancer*. The girl in the movie believed in
Santa Claus and his reindeer. Since her friend didn't
believe, the girl got mad and said nothing was impossible.
She saved Prancer, the reindeer, and he brought her broken
family back together. She and her friend got back together
too.

I know this is a make-believe story, but nothing is
impossible. When I dance, even though I can't hear, I hear
"silent" music in my heart. I believe this silent music comes
from God. Thank you, God, for giving me silent music. . . .

What is silent music? I suppose in the most basic terms it is the residue of music I hear in my hearing aid amplified by my imagination. But why define something so wonderful in basic terms? As Helen Keller said, "One can never consent to creep when one feels an impulse to soar." As a child my spirit wanted to soar, and my hearing aid worked well enough for me to pick up melodies, rhythms, and harmonies. Combined with a heart that yearned to dance and leap and float on air, the music in my heart kept me twirling and pirouetting for hours.

I was so grateful for God's gift of silent music. During the summer between my junior and senior years of high school, I went to Jackson, Mississippi, for a summer workshop conducted by a Christian dance company known as the Ballet Magnificat. I spent two weeks with those devoted dancers and made lots of friends who were very much like me—they loved dancing, and wanted to worship God through ballet. With them I felt like a normal girl. Ballet brought us together, and for those two weeks I was almost able to forget that I had a disability.

When I arrived home, I told my mother that I thought God was calling me to join the Ballet Magnificat as a professional dancer. I would have joined the company immediately after graduation from high school, but my parents kept stressing that education should come first. But college cost money.

We needed financial help, and the scholarships offered through the pageant system seemed a good solution to our financial problem. After all, I had won $1,400 competing for Shelby County Junior Miss. Since I had already been successful in the talent portion of the Junior Miss Pageant and the field of competitors would be smaller, I was reasonably confident that I could do well in the Miss Deaf Alabama Pageant. The experience would be good for me, and might pave the way for other opportunities.

Miss Deaf Alabama Pageant

I was eager to compete again, but looked forward to the Miss Deaf Alabama Pageant for reasons entirely different from those that had excited me about competing for Shelby County Junior Miss. I had so enjoyed my years at CID that I looked forward to being among deaf people again. As Mother and I left for the pageant at the Alabama School for the Deaf in Talledega, I looked at her and grinned. "I always feel left out in the hearing world," I told her, "and now you're going to understand how I feel. You'll feel left out in the deaf world because you don't know sign language."

I was feeling a little devilish, because I truly believed that even my closest family members did not understand how I felt at the most intimate family gatherings. I always felt a little cheated at holiday dinners—every time the family gathered around the dining room table, I missed out on secrets, stories, and punch lines. The situation was not much better at home than it was at school. I grew tired of asking, "What's so funny?" I always felt like a little girl tugging on someone's sleeve and asking, "Will you please repeat that so I can see your lips?" Most of the time when my family gathered to talk, I'd just take a book to the couch and read, or go watch television with my little cousin, Trey. Even in a close family, simple communication can be frustrating for a deaf person.

So I was eager for my mother to understand, through experience, just how isolated and alone I felt. But it wasn't meant to be. When we reached the campus of the Alabama School for the Deaf, we stopped to ask for directions to our dorm. I signed my questions with the sign language I had learned— Signing Exact English—and the deaf man I had stopped couldn't understand me. Most deaf people who sign use American Sign Language, which utilizes a completely different grammar from the sign language I was using.

Here I was, telling my mother how isolated she would feel, and I couldn't even communicate in the language of the deaf! The man tried to answer my question by using a combination of signs and gestures, and my mother understood his gestures and body language better than I did! She thanked him and pointed the way, and I fell silent, frustrated beyond belief. I should have gleaned a lesson from that small encounter—this pageant wasn't going to be the experience I had imagined.

I soon met the six other girls who were my fellow contestants. These girls were completely different from my classmates at CID. These deaf girls did not know how to speak very well, and they definitely looked at me as an outsider.

One of the girls who had spoken to me earlier that night asked why I'd brought my mother. "She doesn't belong here," she bluntly told me, resentment burning in her eyes. "She's a hearing mother, and this is the deaf world."

At the time, I couldn't understand the source of her anger, but now I think I do. Some young children are placed at the Alabama School for the Deaf by hearing families who never really attempt to master sign language. I'm afraid too many of those deaf children grow up thinking that people in the hearing world dislike deaf people. As I looked into that girl's stormy blue eyes, I suddenly realized that though I had often felt frustrated at being left out, my feelings paled in comparison to this girl's anger! Some of these students were completely cut off from their families, not only by physical distance, but also by a failure to communicate.

Before that first night ended, I knew I would never win

that pageant. Most of the girls signed to music for the talent competition, but their motions were simple and detached from the melody, almost like conversation. I was the only one who danced ballet, and to those who couldn't hear the music through their ears or in their hearts, I suppose it must have seemed rather . . . senseless.

The interview portion of the pageant went very badly. All the judges were using American Sign Language, and I could not understand them. The vocabulary for American Sign Language is limited, much smaller than the range of spoken English, and the speakers communicate thoughts instead of complete sentences. So there I was, trying to communicate each word carefully in Signing Exact English—which uses proper English grammar and has a more advanced vocabulary—while the judges stared at me, uncomprehending . . . and frowning.

I wasn't upset when I saw how things were going, in part because this pageant did not offer scholarships to the winner. And it was no surprise when I didn't win or even place as one of the finalists. When the pageant was over, I thanked my family and friends for their support, then went out with the other girls to dinner at a nearby pizza restaurant.

I had hoped we would become friends; instead, I soon found myself becoming embarrassed and ashamed by their actions. Unable to speak and communicate with the hearing world, they insisted upon trying to make the waiter at the restaurant understand sign language. They could have just pointed to the menu to show him what they wanted, but they were adamant about trying to place their orders through sign, and became righteously indignant when the waiter couldn't understand them. I grew tired of the disrespect with which they treated him and finally spoke up, telling the waiter exactly what they wanted. When I did so, I immediately felt them all glaring at me.

For the rest of the evening I was persona non grata at that table. The girls completely ignored me. I felt like I was back in my high school cafeteria, except that the girls who avoided my eyes now were signing, not speaking. I'd ruined their fun and spoiled their method of striking back at the "hearing world."

In a moment of breathless insight, I realized that I, a deaf girl, was being discriminated against by deaf people! Just because I spoke, had a hearing family, danced ballet, and used Signing Exact English, they decided that I could not fit into the deaf culture, that I was not an "ideal" deaf person.

I had always felt alienated from the hearing world.

Now I felt alienated from the deaf world too.

Who Am I?

Mother and I went home to resume our lives, but that pageant left me with an inexplicable feeling of emptiness. Over and over I prayed, "God, who am I? Hearing or deaf? Why do I have to be alone all my life?" Part of me was incredibly sad, another part was angry. Negative thoughts seemed to badger my every waking thought and moment, and I didn't really want to go on living all alone. We humans are social beings, we need each other. Even God is a trinity. . . .

Václav Havel once said, "There are times when we must sink to the bottom of our misery to understand truth, just as we must descend to the bottom of a well to see the stars in broad daylight." I had sunk to the lowest level of my life, and for a while I wasn't sure I wanted to go on living. The future seemed bleak and hopeless, the past nothing but wasted effort.

But God brought me back from the edge of despair by guiding my reading of the Bible. Though I felt isolated from the world, I read what Jesus said to the doubting Thomas, "Blessed are those who haven't seen me and believe." I realized when I read that that *no one* can hear Jesus or see him; *everyone* has to feel him and hear his voice in their hearts. In God's eyes I was just like everyone else. How reassuring! I spent hours in silence, reading my Bible and listening for the voice of God.

And I heard it. Not audibly, but in the same way I hear music in my heart. And Jesus assured me that he loves me, and he will not treat me differently than he treats anyone else. His love confirmed that I was accepted in his sight. By turning to the comfort of my Bible, I came to rest in God's love for me. Though I still didn't know where I'd find a place in this world, I knew that I was in capable hands: God's.

Hearing God's voice in my heart and in his word began opening the whole world to me. One night I looked up at the stars in the sky and noticed that all the stars looked different. Later I discovered that the Bible says that the stars have a different kind of glory than the sun and moon, "and even the stars differ from each other in their beauty and brightness" (1 Corinthians 15:41). But though the stars are different from one another, God is great enough to count the stars and call them all by name! (Psalm 147:4)

That truth is so comforting! Just as God knows the stars, he knows each of us as individuals. God created us each with an infinite number of qualities which make us utterly unique and absolutely different from every other person who has ever existed. We have various talents, abilities, personalities, likes and dislikes; we are all products of a variety of circumstances— different families, nations, races, cultures, and times. And yet God knows us better than we know ourselves. He knows our full potential, and he holds a bright, *realistic* dream for each of us.

As I studied and learned in the silence of my room, I began to understand that my positive attitude—which had evaporated—was not enough to help me find success. I would also have to evaluate my abilities and limitations and set my sights on a realistic dream. What could I become? What could I do with my life? I had no idea, but I decided to trust God for the answers.

Someone once shared an anonymous quote that sums up what I was feeling at that time: "When we walk to the edge of all the light we have and step out into the darkness of the unknown, we must believe that there will be something solid to stand on . . . or that we will be taught how to fly."

I didn't know where or how I was going to fit into the world. But I knew I was honoring my parents by pursuing my education, and that surely pleased God. And I knew I was honoring God's design for me by dancing—I've always known he gave me the desire to praise him through dance. So I knew I had to trust God and keep moving forward. A dream is a journey, and though I wasn't sure where the journey would take me, I knew I'd be shown a solid pathway. And if the path before my feet disappeared, well, that's when I'd learn to fly.

I did know one thing—I wanted to be part of the hearing world, and my family and teachers had worked so diligently with me that I felt truly confident.

While I was still recovering from my experience with the deaf pageant, my mother sat beside me and said, "Heather, I kept you in my world because I love you so much. You belong to our family. You are part of us, not part of the deaf world."

Her words were a help. But I was eighteen, and my world was about to become much larger.

Jacksonville State University

After high school graduation, I chose to go to college at Jacksonville State University in Jacksonville, Alabama, because they offered a special program to mainstream deaf students into regular classes. The program, however, required me to have a sign language interpreter in my classes. I soon found that hearing people who spoke sign language saw the interpreter and assumed that sign language was my preferred means of communication.

I hated it.

Don't misunderstand—there are times when a sign language interpreter makes an important difference. But if a deaf person *relies* upon an interpreter, that interpreter becomes just another wall between the deaf person and the hearing world. I discovered that if a sign language interpreter stands before me, people speak to the interpreter as if I am not even there. They'll say "Ask her if she needs anything" instead of speaking to me. It's not that I dislike sign language, I just want people to communicate directly with me.

One of my goals is to show the world that deaf people are individuals. Marlee Matlin and Helen Keller have been prominently featured using sign language, but not all deaf people sign. I speak, that's part of who I am. I want to show the world that some deaf people can speak, and not just sign.

Jacksonville State University provided the help I needed for college, but my journey to Atlantic City really began the year before I arrived at JSU. While still a senior in high school, I visited the college and went to the recruiting office to meet someone who would show me around the campus. When I stepped into the office, I was struck by the pictures of four very pretty young women on the walls. The young receptionist saw my glance and told me that the women were JSU students who had gone on to win Miss Alabama. "That one," she said, pointing to a beautiful woman's portrait, "is Teresa Strickland, the woman you're waiting to meet. She not only won Miss Alabama, but went on to become first runner-up in the 1979 Miss America Pageant."

Wow, she's so beautiful! I thought. *This woman is really something.* Teresa Cheatham Strickland looked like a model when she stepped out to meet me, and I couldn't believe she was willing to introduce me to JSU. I was immediately impressed by her humble attitude. Though beautiful and charming, she seemed so peaceful and kind.

I could hardly wait to enter Jacksonville State in the fall of 1991. The idea of college thrilled me! I loved all my instructors. They were very helpful. I suppose they were accustomed to having deaf students in class, and they knew it was possible for deaf students to succeed.

But during my first week I found college a little intimidating. I didn't know how to pace myself. I felt the enormous weight of being totally independent and responsible for my own education, health, friendships, and my ballet. Even though I knew college would offer more freedom than I'd known in high school, I wasn't certain how to manage it. How could I ever get all my schoolwork done on time?

Despite my intense desire to succeed, I was plagued by insecurity and doubt. I wasn't sure I could survive in college. One afternoon after I'd just been given a stack of assignments, I fought back tears. I was dead tired because I had lain awake half the night worrying about the day to come. I couldn't stop worrying—had I made a mistake to choose college over an audition for the Ballet Magnificat? Or perhaps I should have chosen to attend Gallaudet, the nation's leading deaf college. Perhaps a deaf girl didn't belong in a hearing college after all. . . .

But after that first week, things settled down. I found that my instructors were willing to help whenever I asked them. I especially loved algebra—mathematics has always been my favorite and best subject—and I didn't need anyone to help me take notes in that class because the problems were all in the textbook. I found life in the dorm a little annoying—my hearing aid picked up all the noises, shrieks, and sounds from the hallway, so it was hard to study—and it felt strange to have a roommate after having my own room at home.

Determined to put forth my best effort in everything, I also began to make friends. Since Mother and Aunt Stephanie had both belonged to sororities, they helped me to understand the value of membership in a fraternal organization. Mother was ZTA, but that group had changed in the years since Mother's membership and I did not feel that organization was right for me.

You see, at that time I didn't know what my future would hold, but I had great faith in God's dream for me and I did not want to do anything to damage the future. My major concern was drinking—I had seen people in the spotlight whose image was tarnished by their actions while under the influence of alcohol. I didn't want to be blown off God's path for me, and I knew anything could happen if I drank or was around people who were drinking.

During rush week I met with representatives from several sororities and always asked one question: "Do you allow underage girls to drink at your functions?" Only one organization told me no: Alpha Omicron Pi. I pledged Alpha Pi, and was immediately caught up in a whirl of sorority activities.

Through my sorority I met Denise, a talented, bright girl who had been at JSU for two years. Denise and I attended the First Baptist Church of Jacksonville together, and I liked the services a lot. I sat in the first row in front of the deaf interpreter, and so was able to understand every word the preacher said.

I had also found a special friend. I had begun to develop a very warm friendship with Fred Bueto, a wonderful Christian gentleman I had met through Baptist Campus Ministries.

Yet, as always, there weren't enough hours in the day for me to do all I needed to do. By the end of November I had decided to turn in my pledge pin and resign from the sorority. Through my association with Denise and Fred, I'd become actively involved with the activities of the Baptist Campus Ministry, and I simply didn't have time for my studies, BCM, and Alpha Pi. And I didn't know that other, even more time-consuming activities lay ahead.

The Possibility Is Planted

No matter what your dream, as you set sail toward the horizon of possibilities, you are going to encounter obstacles. In fact, without the wind to brace your sails and the current to prod the rudder of your ship, you won't go anywhere! One of the keys to success lies in understanding the nature of the obstacle before you, then using it to your advantage. Find out how that obstacle can make you stronger. Learn from it. Grow.

Meeting Teresa Strickland may have turned my thoughts toward the Miss Alabama Pageant, but the idea of competing for Miss America really captured my attention in September 1991. I was home from college for the weekend, and Mother and I watched the televised Miss America Pageant from Atlantic City. Carolyn Sapp won the competition that night, the first Miss Hawaii to win the crown.

The first. The words sparked my imagination.

As the last strains of music died off and the newly crowned Miss America disappeared into a sea of enthusiastic well-wishers, I turned to my mother. "I want to have that opportunity," I told her. "I want to perform my ballet on television. Maybe I can perform on stage and someone from a ballet company or a university with a ballet program will notice me. And I could win scholarship money—"

"Heather," my mother interrupted, "those pageants are for wealthy girls. They cost a lot of money."

"How could they?" I asked. "The contestants are girls who need scholarships, so how could they have a lot of money?"

The voice of inexperience! Mother was right; all pageants cost money. A contestant must buy gowns and a talent costume and hire coaches to help with her talent and prepare for the interview portion of the competition. Plus there's the added expense of transportation to the many places a contestant must go in order to perform community service. Some girls hire professionals to help with makeup and hair, diet and exercise.

I had just felt the first stiff wind of opposition on my dream journey—money.

For an average middle-class family like ours, pageants, even on a local level, were expensive. But my mother saw how committed I was to my dream of dancing, and she agreed to help in any way she could. She began by taking another job, and even worked three jobs during the years I actively competed.

We tried to take financial shortcuts whenever we could. I began by asking other girls if I could borrow their gowns. Most were reluctant to lend their dresses out, and I have to admit that a borrowed gown is not really ideal. A lot of gowns I tried on were not that attractive on me—they just didn't look like *me*. Some had very low-cut necklines that made me feel uncomfortable, others highlighted more of my body than was necessary. In those years, heavy beaded gowns were popular, and I never felt comfortable in those beaded dresses.

Since Stacey has good taste and a flair for fashion, she helped Mother and me with the necessary shopping for gowns, swimsuits, and other clothes. During my first pageant, the Miss St. Clair, Stacey, Mom, and I found a gown on sale. We bought a normal black swimsuit at the mall—one I wouldn't dare wear in a pool—and had to buy black high heels to wear with it. For the interview I wore the same business suit I had worn for the Shelby County Junior Miss Pageant, and for the talent competition I wore my old ballet costume. I felt good about entering this pageant because it didn't cost my mother too much.

Teresa Strickland had advised me to enter the Miss St. Clair Pageant in addition to the Miss JSU Pageant. Earlier in the year I had gone to the office to see her because I missed ballet terribly and thought she might understand my burning desire to praise God through dance. In our first meeting I had sensed the peace of God in Teresa Strickland, and I could see Jesus in her eyes.

Under Teresa's kind and compassionate gaze, I poured out my heart. I told her that I still felt lonely at JSU. I wasn't terribly outgoing and couldn't communicate with my fellow students very well. But pageants had been a way for me to relate and make friends in high school, so why couldn't I compete for the title of Miss JSU?

Teresa sat back, weighing my words, and then asked a simple question: "Heather, what is your talent?"

"I dance ballet."

She smiled—the quiet smile a mother gives a child when she doesn't want to discourage an impossible dream, then she gave me one bit of advice. "You don't have much experience," she said quietly. "Why don't you try out for the Miss St. Clair pageant? It's a smaller pageant than Miss JSU, and the practice will be good for you."

I wasn't crazy about competing in that pageant because I really wanted to win Miss JSU, but I decided to take her advice. Teresa was right—I had never been in a pageant on the Miss America track, and the experience would be good for me.

I learned that Teresa had won the Junior Miss Pageant of her home county, so a few days later I stopped by her office with pictures from the Shelby County Junior Miss Pageant. Teresa took one look at the color photographs of me dancing *en pointe*, then dropped them on her desk, her eyes wide with surprise. "I had no idea," she said, her gaze meeting mine. "I just couldn't picture a deaf girl dancing—until now."

"The music," I explained, pressing my hand to my chest, "is in here. I listen with my heart."

From that moment Teresa and I developed a unique bond. I felt free to be myself around her. She never criticized the things I did, but she corrected me in a positive, honest way. In her I found the person I wanted to be. I wanted to touch people with warmth and love in the same way she did.

And not only did she offer her encouragement, Teresa also volunteered to coach me. I'd never been in a pageant on a par with the Miss St. Clair and the Miss Alabama Pageant, and she helped me understand the interview section and the stage work.

As part of my preparation for the competition, another woman, Jane Rice Holloway, suggested that I travel with her to the Miss Wallace State Pageant, where she was to serve as a judge. Jane had been crowned Miss Alabama in 1973, and I had shared my dreams about a future pageant experience with her.

When we arrived on the campus of Wallace State University, Jane took me to meet Dr. Karen Drinkard, director of the pageant. We met in the dressing room, where all the contestants were bustling about in a flurry of activity.

A shining object caught my eye. The crown, sitting alone in a plain cardboard box, gleamed like a star, and I couldn't help but stare at it. I didn't say a word, but Karen must have seen the dream shining in my eye.

My breath caught in my throat as she looked at me. "You could be the one to wear this," she said, reaching down to pick up the tiara. I couldn't move as she reached forward and placed the crown on my head. *Am I dreaming? Here I am, a deaf girl she doesn't know at all, and she's telling me I could be a winner. . . .*

My cheeks flushed; I wasn't even a contestant. I quickly took the crown off and mumbled something; I didn't want anyone to think that I was plunging ahead with unbridled ambitions.

But even though I gave the crown back, I could still feel its pressure on my head . . . its weight . . . the promise of a dream fulfilled and a starry night to come.

Oh, God, let this dream come true. I'm trying to have a positive attitude, and I think it's a realistic dream. And I'm willing to work very hard. . . .

I did my best to prepare for the upcoming pageant. There were no dance studios on campus, so I found an empty room in the basement of my dorm. It was an ugly room with yellow walls. Tall concrete pillars intersected the designs made by the old floor tiles, but I maneuvered as best I could and danced. The room was so cold, I had to wear a sweater even in the springtime, and I kept falling on that slippery floor. But I practiced ballet for five days a week, two or three hours a day. I grew tired of practicing the same routine over and over and over, but I knew I had to have it down so perfectly that I could do it without thinking. And every day brought me closer to my dream.

A few days later I was staring at another crown . . . the crown destined for the future Miss St. Clair. With Jane Holloway and Teresa Strickland as my encouragers, I was ready to participate in my first pageant on the Miss America circuit. I felt good about my dance, I was fairly confident of my fitness in a swimsuit, and was a little nervous about the interview. My last-minute problems concerned my hair.

My hair is my enemy. My mother loves me to wear it up because an updo makes me look older and more mature. But I

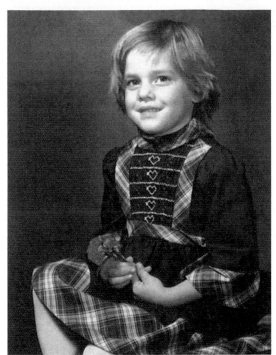

*H*ere *I* am at 4½ years old.

*S*tacey, me, and *M*elissa.

I was 10 years old in this picture, which was taken just a year before *I* left for the school for the deaf.

*Here I am at 12.
I loved sailing and
being on the ocean.*

*I practiced my
"Via Dolorosa"
performance at the
dance studio. Behind
me is my
dance teacher,
Monica Smith.*

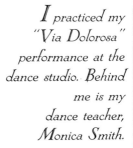

My childhood dream came true as *I* danced the "*Via Dolorosa*" at the *Miss America* pageant in front of millions of people.

My moment of triumph as Miss America. That night almost everyone in the audience was waving the "I love you" sign.

This picture was taken on the night I became Miss America. From left to right: Grandmother, Grandfather, Dad, Stacey, Mother, Melissa, and me at the center.

A month after I won the Miss America pageant, I was at Disney World with the deaf students and Mickey Mouse. We all signed "I love you!"

Bonnie (left) and Mickey (right)— my traveling companions, and my best friends, too!

My first official interview as Miss America took place on "Today" with Bryant Gumbel.

I enjoyed my meeting with Hillary Clinton, who told me to be true to myself, despite all the controversy that was surrounding me at the moment.

My mother and me.

can't put my hair up except in a ballet bun, and a ballet bun doesn't look right with a formal evening gown. I didn't know how to twirl my fine, stubborn hair into a French twist. My hair hates to be up; it's always resisting me.

As time drew near for the Miss St. Clair Pageant, my mother and I argued over my hair while Aunt Stephanie served as referee. I wanted to leave my hair down, Mother kept insisting that I wear it up. The ballet bun was out, so was straight hair. And so we compromised: I wore a plastic banana clip to keep my hair off my shoulders. Though a banana clip is only slightly more dressy than a ballet bun, I suppose Mother figured it was better than wearing my hair down. The clip was easy to snap in, and my mother was happy.

Though my hair problems were solved for the moment, trouble reared its ugly head in the interview room. Because all my life I've been frustrated when sitting with a group of chattering people, I was nervous when I walked into that room. I was afraid I'd have to ask them to repeat their questions and frustrate the judges right into dismissing any chance I might have of success in the pageant.

The three judges gathered around the table weren't my loving relatives either. They were sharp-eyed professionals who didn't know me. I didn't even know if they knew I was deaf, and I wasn't about to tell them.

"Hello, I'm Heather Whitestone, contestant number ten," I announced. Then I sat down and waited for them to ask questions.

One of the judges asked a question while looking down at the table. I couldn't read her lips, and my hearing aid couldn't cut through her heavy Southern accent to pick up her words. The session went from bad to worse as I struggled through my embarrassment and tried to make sense. Here I was, out to prove that a deaf girl could function just like a hearing girl, and I was failing miserably.

Things went steadily downhill on the final night of competition. Teresa Strickland was the emcee at the pageant. Knowing she was nearby gave me peace. I heard her singing as we were backstage changing clothes, and I took a moment to relax and marvel at the purity of her voice.

But during the evening gown competition, when I walked out to answer the question Teresa would ask, my stomach was tied in knots. But I watched Teresa's lips carefully and understood the question: "Heather, who is your favorite dancer, and why?"

"Mikhail Baryshnikov is my favorite dancer," I replied, remembering to smile at the audience. "Because he jumps high."

He jumps high? No other words came to my suddenly blank brain. *He jumps high*, that was it. I clenched my fist, stifling the urge to slap my forehead and groan. The audience stared at me with stupefied looks on their faces; even Teresa seemed stunned. Finally a few members of the audience realized that I had finished, and a light smattering of applause drifted across the auditorium as Teresa thanked me. My cheeks burned as I stepped back into my place in line.

Facing My Limitations

Needless to say, I didn't win the Miss St. Clair Pageant. I wasn't even a finalist. The entire experience had embarrassed me terribly, and I felt like a total failure. Teresa had invested her time to coach me, my mother had worked hard to shell out the money for a new gown, and I'd done all that rehearsing and practice for nothing! I'd done better at the Shelby County Junior Miss Pageant with half the effort.

I didn't win, I told myself, because of my deafness. I couldn't win the Miss Deaf Alabama Pageant because I lived and worked in a hearing world; I couldn't win a hearing pageant because I was deaf. I had done a decent job in the talent, evening gown, and swimsuit competition, but the interview had been a stiff and awkward trial by fire.

I had gone into that interview room wanting to be treated like any other hearing contestant. Trouble was, I was deaf. And I couldn't hear as well as any hearing contestant. But it wasn't my deafness alone that defeated me. It was my inability to master the situation. My family had to help me see the truth and overcome this tremendous obstacle.

The week after the pageant, my family called me into the living room and sat me down for a sorely needed pep talk. The Miss JSU Pageant was only two weeks away, and I was beginning to wonder if I should even bother showing up.

Tom Vera, Stacey's husband, gave me a wonderful piece of advice. "Heather," he said, looking me straight in the eye, "look at the interview portion of the competition as a job interview. You've got to sell yourself. You've got to convince them that you can handle the job of being Miss Jacksonville State University."

Convince the judges? I wasn't certain I could convince myself.

Stacey's advice came next: "Heather, first of all, you need to have fun with this. If you don't enjoy the pageants, then you're not doing the world or yourself any good. If you can participate and enjoy it, go for it! But if the experience isn't fun, just don't do it."

Finally it was Mother's turn. "Heather, the judges were awkward because you didn't tell them how to communicate with you. They need to know they must look at you when they're speaking to you. Tell them to talk slowly. You can't expect them to automatically know how to communicate with you. If the barriers are going to fall, you're going to have to make the first move in taking them down."

Fortified like that, how could I help but continue on? I had to face my problems and understand them. I had to learn from them and grow. I had to be honest with the judges . . . and with myself.

I went to work right away. Janet White, one of my professors, spent a lot of time working with students with disabilities, and I trusted her instincts. In her private office Janet and I had many conversations about God and our relationship with Jesus. One day I had a disagreement with a close friend, and Janet gave me good advice.

"Heather, I could hold up a quarter right now," she said, holding up an imaginary coin. "And I could say 'I see a man's head' while you could insist that you see an eagle. We'd both be one hundred percent sure that we were right, and right we would be because we were looking at the coin from two different perspectives. Instead of wasting time in an argument, it is better to try to see things from the other person's perspective."

I never forgot Janet's advice, and I started to look at my interview from the judges' perspective. How could I make things easier for them? And how could I prepare myself to answer their questions? I asked Janet to help me with the troublesome interview, and she agreed to help me become up-to-date on current issues. She also enlisted a history professor, who quizzed me about world affairs, government, and politics. These two ladies helped me practice by asking impromptu questions in an interview setting. Even Fred, my boyfriend at the time, quizzed me when I wasn't in class or working with the professors. By the end of those two weeks I felt very confident.

College students have a tendency to concentrate on classwork and fun, forgetting everything else, but by the time the Miss JSU Pageant came around, I was very aware of what was going on in the world. I didn't expect to win. I decided to take my family's advice: I would treat the interview as seriously as if

I were applying for a job, and I would have fun with everything else. I loved the dancing and dressing-up involved in a pageant, and I told myself I could learn to like the interviews too.

As I waited outside the interview room for my appointment, I looked at my fellow contestants, who were also waiting. Their faces were tight with anxiety, some of them nervously jiggled their legs, looking as scared as if they were going to court. *Why are they scared? The judges aren't going to bite them.* Some of them were actually moving their lips, silently practicing the answers to questions they thought they'd be asked.

I was so relaxed, I almost didn't care. The voice of God spoke to my heart: "Just be yourself, Heather, be natural, and they will take you seriously." And this time I listened.

When I entered the interview room, I greeted the judges with a smile, just as though they were old friends. I walked to the empty chair, sat down, and looked each of them in the eye one at a time, and followed my mother's advice.

"Hello, I'm Heather Whitestone," I said. "And I'm deaf. But I read lips, so if you speak slowly and look at me when you talk, I'll be able to understand what you're saying. This will be a piece of cake, so don't worry. If I can't understand you, you can write the question on a piece of paper and I'll be happy to answer it."

As one, they smiled. My honesty had put them—and me—at ease. They appreciated my honesty and opened their hearts to me. We had a wonderful interview, we laughed, we were like friends having a regular conversation. I believe it was the best interview I ever had, even better than the one I had during the Miss America Pageant.

The question I remember most distinctly is "Heather, how do you feel about children being given condoms in public school?"

Without stopping to think I said, "School is a place where

children should learn not to have sex!" My opinion was so strong, my voice must have rung out like a politician's. They laughed and nodded their heads. At that point, whether they agreed with me or not, I knew I had won their hearts.

The rest of the competition was a breeze. I was so relaxed, I took a nap while waiting for my turn to dance. I wasn't nervous at all, I just did my best, and was pleasantly surprised when I won the talent competition.

On the final night, when it was time for the emcee, Teresa Strickland, to announce the winners, Teresa made a mistake. She announced the fourth runner-up, then realized she had forgotten to announce the talent and swimsuit winners. She apologized to the crowd, then said, "The talent winner is Heather Whitestone. She will receive one semester's free tuition."

I hadn't heard a word of her explanation. Since she'd announced the fourth runner-up and everyone was applauding and looking at me, I thought I was third runner-up. I smiled and walked down to stand beside the fourth runner-up and waited for someone to bring me flowers.

Miss JSU 1991 hurried over to me, took my hand, and led me back to my place in line. I was so confused—I wanted to hide my face behind the curtain, but I had to stand there as Teresa went on to announce the swimsuit winner. That's when I realized what had happened.

When she finally announced the name of Miss JSU, I looked at the other girls' faces. They were all looking at me, and the girl behind me tapped my shoulder.

I took a quick breath of utter astonishment as a feeling of glorious happiness sprang up in my heart. Me. I had won.

I walked down to center stage and felt the weight of the crown as it was placed on *my* head. Joy bubbled in my laugh and shone in my eyes. As I found my family in the crowd and waved to them, I was amazed to see the audience rise to its feet in a standing ovation for me.

Even then I wasn't thinking about Miss America or even Miss Alabama. I was thinking that being Miss JSU would open doors and introduce me to people on campus. I had earned scholarship money to continue my education, and perhaps I could finally broaden my social life and make more friends. This was the pageant I had cared about most.

When I finally returned to the dorm that night, I placed the Miss JSU crown on my dresser before the mirror, steeling myself for the bigger step ahead. I'd have to cultivate a desire to become Miss Alabama, perhaps even Miss America. Quite frankly, I wasn't very mature in that pageant, because I kept giddily thinking, "So this is how it feels to be a beauty queen." I hadn't thought much about being a role model, but at least I had chosen to dance to a song, "How Beautiful," that would be a witness for Jesus. That night was simply the fulfillment of a little girl's dream.

The Miss JSU pageant introduced me to the college. After that night, more students recognized my name, and, buoyed by new confidence, I became a little more outgoing. I made a few new friends, but winning Miss JSU strengthened my desire to move upward. I entered the Miss Alabama Pageant three months after winning Miss JSU, and took my pageant work so seriously that I focused on little else during my college years.

Miss Alabama

Now that I had made my first successful step on the "pageant trail," I decided to enter the Miss Alabama Pageant. The experience was nothing like the other pageants I'd entered. It was almost like being part of a college football team; the audience really took the "sport" seriously! The entire state, it seemed to me, wanted to sponsor a winner, someone who would proudly represent them before the nation at the Miss America Pageant.

The other contestants were kind and helpful to me during the pageant week. Since I was not able to hear clearly or read the lips of whoever talked to us from a distance, my fellow contestants let me know what was going on. Some contestants were "rookies" like me. Others had competed for the title of Miss Alabama before, and they seemed more serious about the competition.

During the Miss Alabama Pageant I became aware of the importance of a contestant's platform and community service. Since 1989, Miss America has become a spokesperson for whatever platform she selects. She travels across the country on a national speaking tour during her year of service, giving hundreds of speeches about her chosen area of concern. Likewise, Miss Alabama contestants were working hard on their community service platforms. I realized that whoever became Miss Alabama would not only have a chance to win greater scholarships, but also travel throughout Alabama on a speaking/entertaining tour. My heart skipped a beat when I thought about the possibility of dancing for audiences across Alabama all year long!

On my first attempt to win the Miss Alabama Pageant, I finished as first runner-up. God knew I wasn't ready to move on . . . not yet. But I was happy and honored to be the first runner-up. That night I made a plan—I would work hard in order to come back to the Miss Alabama Pageant the next summer. My desire to win the Miss Alabama crown just grew stronger.

But the second year was more difficult. The students at JSU now knew my name and I was no longer in the isolation that had helped me prepare for my first success. I could have spent my time involved in social activities, but I nonetheless chose to stay focused on the Miss Alabama crown. For my preliminary pageant, I entered and won Miss Point Mallard in Decatur, Alabama, just two weeks after the Miss Alabama Pageant. Decatur is a two- or three-hour drive from Jacksonville, so I spent a few weekends there doing public appearances. Every weekend I wasn't in Decatur I drove one and a half hours to Monica Smith's dance studio in Birmingham. And every day during the school year I watched the TV news, trying to stay informed about current events so I'd be prepared for the interview competition.

My spare time, what little I had, was spent organizing and performing community service. I volunteered to accompany deaf and hearing choirs to various locations in order to perform sign language to songs they sang. As we performed, I remember seeing smiles on wrinkled faces at nursing homes, happy children at elementary schools, and appreciative audiences at churches and the Alabama School for the Deaf.

But being a leader in community service is a lot like being a football quarterback. Some players don't want to follow you, and lots of folks in the stands will question your decisions! Some of the students I was trying to "lead" in a certain project didn't want to follow, and I struggled with what I felt were their disrespectful attitudes toward me. I considered quitting my community service altogether, but I wanted to be Miss Alabama and knew community work was extremely important.

So again I went to my professor Janet White for advice. Janet reminded me that no one would ever agree with me about everything, and just because I was a leader didn't mean I was completely in charge. In order to achieve my goals, I had to treat the people I worked with as if we were all part of a team. I had to give them responsibilities, and then trust them to fulfill them. "If you want to be a great leader," she told me, "be a great servant."

I thought she was kidding. How can a leader be a servant? Doesn't being a leader mean being the *boss*?

"Dear God," I prayed in my dorm room that evening, "how can I be a servant? How can I trust others to do what they're supposed to? What if they don't do the right thing?"

God brought me to the Bible. In Matthew 23:11–12 I read, "The greatest among you must be a servant. But those who exalt themselves will be humbled, and those who humble themselves will be exalted."

Then I read of how Jesus, God's perfect and beloved son, washed the feet of his lowly disciples. In my heart, a quiet voice reminded me of something I'd heard once: "The greatest achievements are those which benefit others. Nobody really cares how much you know until they see how much you care."

I went back to my fellow students and apologized for being bossy. I asked them to help me achieve our goal of building a bridge between the hearing and deaf worlds. I gave them the responsibility of handling their own jobs. I motivated them to achieve their goals instead of telling them what to do. And to my surprise, they all had a great time and the job got done. It took a little work—and a lot of humbling—for me to learn to be a leader!

Meanwhile, Teresa Strickland was still serving as my volunteer coach. She especially helped me with mock interviews, still my weak spot. She urged me to take my stuffed animals and pretend they were judges. In the privacy of my dorm room I practiced talking to their faces, tried not to say "umm," and disciplined myself not to kick my leg nervously or twiddle my fingers. Fortunately, I loved stuffed animals, and it was easy to prepare for interviews with them. I had no problem talking to toys that didn't talk back!

When I returned to the Miss Alabama Pageant, I didn't have as much fun as I'd had the first time. Most of the contestants I met the year before came back. This time we were feeling more competitive because we were eager to win the title. And this time I was dancing to a new song, "Via Dolorosa," which was a more difficult ballet routine. I was not quite ready for that ballet performance, and the only thing that got me through the talent portion were my dance teacher's words of encouragement. Monica Smith, my dance instructor, had been a contestant in the Miss Alabama Pageant herself, and had won the talent competition for three years. She was also a Christian, so I enjoyed talking to her about faith.

But still I was nervous during the second Miss Alabama Pageant. I was taking it all too seriously. I keenly felt the pressure to win—because I had been first runner-up the year before, almost everyone expected me to win this time. And I had worked so hard, neglecting my social life completely. . . . Surely God would reward me with the crown.

When the emcee was about to announce the first runner-up, my heart said, "It's you."

Shut up. I don't want to hear it. I don't want to finish in second place again.

"The first runner-up is Miss Point Mallard, Heather Whitestone!"

No, not me!

As I walked to get my flowers and take the first runner-up's position—for the second time—I thought, "How can I do this? How can I come so close and not win? What is wrong with me?"

At that point I began to question my ability to succeed. Were the judges doubting my ability to handle the job of Miss Alabama? Didn't they believe a deaf woman could handle the job? I did not voice these thoughts for a long time because I didn't want to believe them.

That night I decided I wouldn't attempt to win Miss Alabama a third time. I didn't want to be first runner-up again. I wanted a social life, I wanted to rest, I wanted freedom.

I held my anger and tears in my heart. As a photographer shot pictures of the winner and the runners-up, I gave him a fake smile and tried to act like a lady.

But when I saw my family and friends, my faithful support team, I exploded into sobs. I didn't want to cry in front of them because I didn't want their pity. But it was too late. My heart was too weak to hold the tears back.

I went through a season of disappointment. I had worked so hard, and though I know now that the effort taught me to be disciplined and my community service had touched the lives of others, I couldn't see the benefits of all my hard work.

But often we have no idea how we are touching other people's lives. After that second Miss Alabama Pageant, I received a letter from a woman who had been in the audience and seen my dance. "I wanted you to know that a deaf man came to me looking for a job," she wrote. "I didn't know whether or not I should hire him until I saw you onstage. I watched how you mastered your situation and overcame your problems. I really admired your efforts, and because of your example, I decided to hire the deaf man and give him a chance."

Even if you think you will never reach your dream, remember that you will learn something and touch others on the journey.

One Final Attempt

I participated in the Miss Alabama Pageant three times. Success didn't come easily, but along the way I learned that being Miss America is a very serious job. During the Christmas holidays in my second year of preparing for the Miss Alabama Pageant, Teresa gave me a book that I read all through Christmas vacation. In it I found the following quote from Colleen Kay Hutchins.

> Tell the girl who wins the title this year to remember that she only borrows the crown for a year. Tell her she doesn't create it, and tell her every Miss America who has gone before has added to it a jewel. Tell her she is taking on a great responsibility. A responsibility to herself, to her people, to the Miss America Pageant, the people of Atlantic City, her state and her nation. Tell her the country and the world will judge America by her.

I memorized this quote, and repeated it to myself every morning that I served after finally winning Miss Alabama 1994. And I continued to work hard—at my dance, my studies, and my community service. I knew I could improve in all three areas.

I was occasionally asked to give speeches to motivate young people, but when I asked them afterward what they'd learned, I usually got blank looks for an answer. My quest to help students led me to establish my pageant platform, my STARS program (Success Through Action and Realization of your dreamS).

With the help of my family and friends, I identified five guiding principles that helped me find success. Stacey and Tom Vera, my sister and brother-in-law, came up with the idea of likening these principles to the five points of a star. I often used my crown to demonstrate the five points, but because the crown has only four points, the fifth point had to be represented by me . . . or you!

The first point is *have a positive attitude*. God gives each of us a similar heart and brain, yet we are all unique and special. One child will excel and flourish, another will settle for second best and "coast" through life. What is the difference? A positive attitude. I believe we should celebrate our uniqueness, identify our strengths, and build upon those.

As I began to compete, I worried about my voice—would people understand me when I introduced myself on the pageant stage? My voice is a little different, in fact, one time I was in a restaurant where a French waiter heard me speak, then looked at me in surprise. "Are you from France?" he asked, lifting an eyebrow. "I'm French! You have a French accent!"

Wow. I have a French accent, and I've never even taken French lessons!

By joking about my voice, I tried to put a positive light on my experiences, even though I wondered if Americans would want a "Miss America sweetheart" with a French accent!

Ray Bradbury, the best-selling science fiction author, offers this key to success: "Love what you do—and do it!" And Jack Goeken, founder of the MCI telephone network, urges people to "believe that nothing is impossible. It doesn't matter how many times you fail in trying to get something to work. All you need is one success."[1] I like those positive attitudes!

Failure comes to all of us, but I believe a negative attitude is the worst handicap in the entire world. When I experience failure, I cannot blame God or fate or circumstances—usually my own negative attitude is responsible. Sometimes we fail because we fail to plan, sometimes we attempt to fulfill our dreams before we have adequately prepared for the challenge. Sometimes God allows us to fail at one endeavor in order to lead us into another. But we can survive even what seems to be disastrous failure as long as we preserve our positive, faith-filled attitude.

The second point is to *have a dream.* Education is a worthy

---

[1]Ray Bradbury and Jack Goeken quoted in Derric Johnson's, *Easy Doesn't Do It* (Y.E.S.S. Press, 1991), pp. 158–59.

dream, so is achievement. I did not find success in pageants because I was deaf, but because I worked and studied diligently. I encourage young people not to drop out of high school, but to continue to study and work toward their dreams, taking one step at a time.

John H. Johnson, publisher of *Ebony* magazine, tells people to start with small dreams. "Set short-term goals," he says. "Great dreams are often so far away from your reach that you can become discouraged. But each small goal you achieve gives you confidence to try the next."[2]

Sometimes our dreams can change, and this is nothing to be discouraged by. For my first three years of college I was determined to be an accountant, but later I was considering a career in business administration. As I write this, I'm not certain where my future dreams will lead, but I'm confident I will keep pressing on. I am at a different place in my life, but I'm still seeking God's will for my life. So I know tomorrow holds another exciting, fulfilling dream.

The third point in the STARS program is *a willingness to work hard*. We all have to work hard. I wish I hadn't had to deal with my mother talking with her lips hidden behind her hand so that I'd learn to depend upon my hearing aid. But now I'm glad I did. And I learned because we worked hard together.

There were times in my life when I cried out to the Lord, saying, "Lord, why did you make things so hard for me?" But God reminded me that there is a reason for every problem. The troubles and tests were sent to make me stronger and to teach me to depend upon God when my strength wasn't enough. If God calls you to a task, you should prepare with every ounce of energy within you.

Bill Rosenburg, founder of Dunkin' Donuts, says that suc-

---

[2]Ibid., p. 158.

cess is found when people work "can't see" hours: "Start work when it's so dark you can't see and finish when you can't see because it's dark again."[3] In other words, work hard and work long!

Someone once told me a Bible story that illustrates this point: David, king of Israel, wanted to make a sacrifice to God. He sent a messenger to Araunah, a man who owned a site suitable for a sacrifice, and offered to buy Araunah's threshing floor. "Why should the king pay for my threshing floor?" Araunah asked. "I'll give him whatever he needs—even the oxen and my sledges for the wood."

"No, I insist upon buying it," David answered when he was told of Araunah's reply. "I cannot present offerings to the Lord that have cost me nothing."

Do you see the point of the story? We serve God by serving others, and everything we do, whether we are going to school, taking care of children, or laboring in an office, is work done for the Lord. If you want to offer your hard work to the Lord, it must cost something—your time, your dedication, your effort, your energy. Anything worth doing is worth doing well.

Your dreams will require hard work. And the harder you work, the more you will appreciate them.

The fourth point is to *face your limitations*. I had to face my limitations in order to become Miss America—remember all those interview practice sessions? I had to face an entirely new set of limitations as Miss America and yet another set when I surrendered my crown. I'm beginning to think that every phase of life comes with its own challenges!

However, facing your limitations doesn't mean that you should set lower goals for yourself because of the obstacles you run up against. But you must confront them realistically in

---

[3]Ibid., p. 158.

order to conquer them. One doesn't overcome a limitation by pretending it doesn't exist.

After I surrendered my Miss America crown, I was on my own and more than a little scared. I had to take care of my own business, and I'd never done anything like that in my life. I had no idea what the future held for me. People from all over the country were still calling me to arrange speaking engagements and appearances, and I had no secretary, no one to help me keep track of financial arrangements, no one to plan my schedule. I had to face my problem and admit that I needed help—lots of it. After a few disastrous experiences, I finally hired a speaker's bureau to handle those arrangements for me.

We have to learn from our mistakes. William Dean Singleton, co-owner of MediaNews Group, Inc., says that too many people keep stubbornly plowing ahead and repeating their mistakes. "I believe in the motto 'try and try again,' " he says. "But the way I read it, it says 'try, then stop and think. Then try again.' "[4]

We all have obstacles in our lives, but as I've said, I have found tremendous inspiration in the example of Helen Keller. An Alabama native like me, Helen was both deaf and blind, and was dismissed as being completely unteachable for the early part of her life. She had more obstacles than I have ever had, but she amazes me with her wisdom. She couldn't hear spoken words or see them in books, yet she wrote beautiful stories. "Know your problems, but don't let them master you," she often said. "Let them teach you patience, sweetness, and kindness, because you never know what miracles you will make in other people's lives or in your life."

As I write this, I have just returned from a speaking engagement for Alabama Power, the electric utility company. While

---

[4]Ibid., p. 159.

I was there, Elmer Harris, the company CEO, surprised me with a gift—a financial contribution to establish the Heather Whitestone Foundation for the purpose of helping others reach their dreams. While I stood on the platform in silent surprise and joy, I listened to the CEO tell a story that took my breath away. A woman in his company had seen me waiting in an airport two years before, and something I had done as Miss America had moved her so dramatically that she repeated the story to company officials. The result? They were moved to help me establish this charitable foundation.

On that day two years earlier, I had no idea that my actions would mean anything to anyone other than myself and a sick girl I met in the Atlanta airport. We were waiting for a plane that had been delayed, and by some quirk of fate I was carrying my crown in its little wooden box. The sick girl, who was sitting at the gate in a wheelchair, recognized me, and her mother came over to speak to me. I don't remember all of the conversation, but somehow I felt moved to take the crown out of the box and place it on the girl's head.

She was pleased, I was happy to do it, and I thought that was the end of the story. But as that corporate executive from Alabama Power told me the story, I learned that other people watching in that airport had been moved to tears. Such a little gesture, and yet it meant so much! That's one of the wonderful things about following God on our dream journey. You never know how God is going to use you!

Though you may not be aware of it, I'm sure you have made a difference in someone else's life. The teachers who gave me an education, my family members who sacrificed their own time and energy in order to help me—they all brought miracles to my life. I couldn't have won Miss America without the help and support of many people who took the time—who *made* the time—to help me become an example of the STARS program.

Thinking of those people brings me to the fifth and final point of the STARS program: *Develop and use an effective support system.* I don't believe anyone can be happy and successful without a support team. My family was the strongest part of my support team. They helped me look at my problems from different perspectives. Instead of pitying me, they challenged me to do my best.

Your support team is made up of people who will remind you that you can do anything with God's help. Your team members may be your parents, your teachers, people from your church or synagogue, anyone who has an impact in your life. If you don't have a support team, make friends with people who hold your values and can share your dreams.

My support team extended far beyond my family. I could never have made my dreams come true without the help of many people, including Vicki and Jim Davis, their daughter, Donnalee Davis Blankenship, and her husband, Brandon Blankenship. I met this wonderful family through my experience with the Shelby County Junior Miss Pageant. Donnalee had won that pageant several years before my participation, and the Davises were ardent supporters of the program because they believed in supplying scholarships for young women.

When the Davises heard that I was going to compete for the Miss Alabama title, they came to support me at that first pageant. During the second year, we held mock interviews in their house, with Vicki, Jim, Donnalee, and Brandon serving as "judges." When I became first runner-up again, they all saw my discouragement and despair. Still believing that I could succeed, they gave me an airplane ticket to Atlantic City. Brandon said I should tell the judges that a deaf lady is more than equipped to handle the job. "Tell them that you know they are wondering if a profoundly deaf woman can handle the job of Miss America. Tell them, 'Yes, I can.' "

Brandon's encouragement made a difference. It allowed me to motivate the judges to believe in me. And it motivated me to concentrate on my *abilities*, not my disability.

I think God was speaking to Vicki and Jim; I *know* he was speaking to me while I was in Atlantic City. As I mingled in the crowds outside the hall where the pageant is held, a man known as Boardwalk Bob was selling pageant cards in front of the convention hall. I'd never met him before, and I'm sure he had no idea I was deaf, but he stopped hawking his wares for a moment, looked me straight in the eye, and said, "You come back next year. You'll be Miss America."

I was hearing that refrain everywhere. Karen Drinkard, the director of the Miss Cullman Pageant, had told me earlier, "You could be a winner." She later added, "Think Miss America, not Miss Alabama."

I was also encouraged by Virginia McDorman, a judge of the Miss Cullman area pageant. She told me that as soon as she saw me walk into the interview room, she knew I would be the next Miss America. "You just glowed when you walked into that room," she told me later. "I knew I was looking at the next Miss America."

Karen Drinkard, Boardwalk Bob, Virginia McDorman, and hundreds of others encouraged me. Their words were like oxygen to my soul, and reminded me of a Bible verse I had found: "It is wonderful to say the right thing at the right time!" (Proverbs 15:23)

The first time I'd won first runner-up in the Miss Alabama contest, Teresa Strickland gave me a book about Miss Americas and inscribed it with the words "It is my dream that you will be one of them." Her quiet faith had such an impact on me. I wanted to believe in her dream, I wanted to live up to everyone's expectations. I especially wanted to be like Teresa Strickland. I didn't covet her title or her job, but her heart. I knew she was the kind of woman America needs.

This Is Your Time

My mother and Aunt Stephanie were with me for the 1994 Miss America Pageant. After Kimberly Aiken, Miss South Carolina, had been crowned, I went to the reception room to congratulate our Miss Alabama, Kalyn Chapman, for the fine job she'd done. After an hour or two of mingling, Mother, Stephanie, and I were ready to walk back to the hotel, but we paused inside the empty convention hall. The workers were cleaning the auditorium, picking up trash, and putting chairs away. I asked one man, "Do you mind if I walk on the stage?"

"Who cares?" he said, shrugging. "Go ahead."

With no one to see me but Aunt Stephanie and the workers, Mother and I climbed up onto the stage and turned toward the runway. I looked out at the empty space—as large as two football fields—and suddenly felt confident and relaxed.

In an instant, all my old insecurities vanished. I felt the presence of God right there beside me, and he spoke to my heart: *Go back and continue with your hard work, this is the time for you, this year.*

I didn't know then if I would be Miss America, I just knew I was supposed to work toward Miss Alabama with renewed energy. I thought God wanted me to witness for Jesus on whatever stage I found myself. In his wisdom, I don't think God wanted me to know I would be Miss America. If I'd known, maybe I wouldn't have worked so hard, or maybe I'd have become snobby. God wanted me to depend upon him completely, to have complete trust in his plan.

Once we got home, I began to work harder and study God's word with new zeal. Only God knew what was best for me, where I would fit into the world. And I trusted him to bring my dreams into line with his dreams for me.

As the competition drew near, Teresa sent me a card with

one simple message: "Heather, stay focused on Jesus. When you're competing in the pageant, keep your focus on him. If you lose your focus, you will not get through the tough situations. So follow Jesus in your heart, don't let gossip or the audience or a mistake you might make control you. Only Jesus. Let him rule in your heart."

It wasn't easy to stay focused because I was completely exhausted from pageant preparation. I had transferred to the University of Montevallo, which had a great accounting program, but no one there knew me. Worse yet, that university did not adequately meet my needs for communication, and I struggled to keep my grades up. I was dancing two or three hours a day, six days a week. I had very few chances to meet new people and no time for social activity. I spent my only spare time at the Green Valley Elementary School doing community service. I still watched the TV news and read the newspaper every day.

But all the hard work was worth it, because that year I won the Miss Alabama title. I knew within a few months I'd be standing on that Atlantic City stage once again.

Teresa Strickland was emcee again that last night of the Miss Alabama Pageant. When she began to announce the winners, I tensed and experienced a gamut of emotions. The title "first runner-up" was my enemy. It was a title I didn't want again.

Teresa went through the procedure, and I smiled and tried not to let my emotions show on my face. It was time for Teresa to announce the first runner-up, and I steeled myself not to look in her direction. I watched the audience, waiting for someone to tap my shoulder . . . but no one touched me. Another contestant walked to the front and stood in the spot where I'd stood for the last two years. At that moment I felt a sudden sinking feeling—almost like a kid who has to welcome a new baby sister but feels that somehow she's been displaced.

Then the girl next to me grabbed my hand. From the corner of my eye I could see other contestants staring at me.

Dear God, tell me what is going on. . . .

Teresa announced the winner; the audience went wild. I couldn't hear the name through the eruption of noise, but the girl next to me turned and said, "You won. Heather, you won!"

I suddenly felt so cold and dizzy, I thought I would faint. I'd worked so hard, but all at once I thought I couldn't manage that short walk up to accept the crown. Such a responsibility! It had taken so much for me to win Miss Alabama, how could I hope to represent my home state at the Miss America Pageant?

Heather, I am still with you.

I listened to my heart. God spoke clearly, and he gave me the joy and encouragement I needed to walk forward and accept the crown.

Bound for Atlantic City

The Miss America Pageant is like the Olympics, except that only one person wins each year. Once you win a state title, you can't come back. Dwelling on the once-in-a-lifetime significance of the pageant might have made me a little nervous, but I was very calm during the week of Miss America competition—it was almost an eerie calm. I simply trusted God and focused on Jesus. That was unusual for me, I had never approached any of my other pageants with this level of calm. I felt like for the past three years I had been spinning through a typhoon at sea, and now I had reached the smooth bay where sailing was effortless. The voice in my heart said, "Don't worry, Heather, I'm in charge. Relax. Dance for me."

And so I did. During the week of preliminary competition, I did my best. I admit I was scared to death when I had an interview with the five judges. Right before I walked into the room, I felt my stomach tying itself into knots. The interview competition was still my toughest obstacle. I had only one chance, and that would soon be gone. I was fighting back tears. My heart kept telling me to relax, but I couldn't. I tried my best to be myself, but when I left the room, I felt disappointed.

It was easier to relax during practice sessions. During one break on the convention center stage, I sat down on the floor and looked at the dark, yawning space where the audience would sit. I thought of all the struggles my family and I had endured when I was growing up. I thought about Mother having faith enough to enroll a deaf girl in dance class, and Dad teaching me how to ride a bicycle so I could learn to be independent and leave the house. I remembered Granddaddy Gray teaching me how to use a sense of humor to see the positive side of any problem, and Stacey helping me to prepare for pageants. I saw Melissa being my best buddy in childhood and Aunt Stephanie helping Mother and me to reach a compromise about my stubborn hair.

Tears sprang up in my eyes, and my heart overflowed with joy and gratitude. I thanked God for my family, and for the simple miracle of making it to the Atlantic City stage. The feeling in my heart at that moment overshadowed by far the moment of winning the crown. Sitting alone on that stage, I cried more than I did in the crowning moment when I was surrounded by a horde of excited friends.

We had several rehearsals before the final night of competition. During one of our rehearsals of the final segment I found myself staring at the crown in fascination. During the rehearsal, they use an assistant to the dance choreographer to stand in for the winner, and they use a "rehearsal crown."

More than anything, I wanted to touch that crown. It's an unspoken rule that contestants shouldn't touch the crown, but after they practiced "crowning" the dancer's assistant, I reached out and helped her take the crown out of her hair.

"Oh, no," one of the hostesses good-naturedly fussed at me, "whoever touches this crown will be the next Miss America."

I'd already touched it. My heart beat faster as my head flooded with visions of what that crown could mean to me. That crown would give me a bigger voice to encourage people to follow the dreams God has given them. That crown would enlarge my witness for Jesus. I could influence America and remind people what a wonderful country God has given us.

I had been thinking a lot about how most people seemed to have forgotten about God and his goals for them. I had seen so many unhappy people! I had a great desire to serve God, and that crown would give me a bigger voice to encourage people to take God seriously and to lift their eyes above their ordinary tasks. I wanted to urge them to stop and think about the Creator . . . the one who made us and inspires our dreams.

When the final night of competition began, I discovered that I wanted to dance for God. Not for the Miss America crown, despite my great desire to win. God was far more important than the crown.

I didn't know if I'd win, and I didn't care. All I wanted to do was dance to "Via Dolorosa" on national television. The song and my ballet dance vividly portray Christ's agony and great love as he climbed Calvary to die for the sins of the world, and I prayed that I would simply have a chance to dance on national television.

After I won Miss Alabama, someone had told me that if I wanted to be Miss America, I'd have to find another song— that Christian music wouldn't win the crown. I thought a lot about that comment. God is very powerful. He made the earth, grass, trees, water—everything I loved. He also made people and their brains. If God wanted me to be Miss America, he could certainly lead the judges in their decision. So I decided to ignore that comment and use Christian music. First and foremost, I wanted to glorify God through my dance.

The little girl's dream had changed. Now I wanted to glorify God not as a prima ballerina, but as a Miss America contestant. I'd actually have the potential to dance before more people on this *one night* than I would if I'd had a lifelong career of dancing as the world's most famous ballerina.

The night began, the TV cameras began to blink, the cavernous hall filled with thousands of people. My fellow contestants and I were running on adrenaline, and yet I still felt that strange, perfect peace that had sustained me through the week.

My name was called as a semi-finalist. I wasn't too surprised, since on Wednesday night I had won the preliminary swimsuit competition, and on Thursday I had won the talent preliminary. However, I was honored that I had been given the opportunity to be a top ten finalist.

Thank you, God. I will dance for you on television.

A giddy thought buzzed about in my brain. Sandi Patty, the artist who recorded "Via Dolorosa," had sent word that she would watch me on TV. I was about to dance before a TV audience of forty million people, and all I could think was "Oh, my goodness, Sandi Patty is watching me."

My childhood dream was about to come true. I danced, not by feeling the vibrations, but by learning the music through my hearing aid, then counting beats and setting my ballet movements to the rhythms. Near the end of "Via Dolorosa" I had to do a series of rapid turns. It is a difficult progression, a dancer must imagine herself to be a playing card so that her entire body turns all at once. If I somehow moved my head before my body, or vice versa, I would lose my balance.

I had a tendency to make mistakes in that section, in fact, during the preliminary talent competition I didn't turn properly. There was a step at the back of the performing area, and I lost my balance and nearly tumbled over the back step.

But on the night I danced for America, God told me to relax. When I came to that series of turns, I could have sworn that an angel was pushing my shoulder forward, providing the momentum I needed to remain straight and keep going. I just stood there and spun.

I've never felt anything like that before or since. My dance was timed to be two minutes and thirty seconds, but that night I thought someone had hurried the tape, I danced for what felt like only half a minute at most. When I finished, during the bows, I saw the applauding crowd and told myself, *This is it. This is what you have been working for three hours a day, five days a week, for over two years. Now it's over.*

I couldn't exactly define the feeling. Sometimes at points of great sorrow or elation our minds go blank, and that's how I felt at that moment. I had just fulfilled one of my greatest dreams, and I didn't know whether to feel happiness or sorrow.

But there was no time to contemplate. The competition was continuing: evening wear, interviews, and the final scoring were yet to come. I hurried offstage to change yet again, and murmured a prayer that God would keep helping me to do my best.

After the talent competition, I paused backstage in my little area of the dressing room. I had narrowed my choices of evening gowns to two: a gorgeous glittery gold gown that was so striking, it could practically win a beauty pageant by itself, and a more simple white gown. Everybody I had asked liked both gowns, and though I really thought the gold gown was more beautifully dramatic, I thought the judges would see my heart better in the white gown. Ann Northington, my dressmaker, mentioned that the white gown might remind them of my dance, where I'd worn a white costume. And so I chose to wear the white gown so the world could see my heart and listen to my message.

The rest of the pageant flew by like a dream. Before I knew it, I stood before the TV cameras as one of five finalists. Regis Philbin, who hosted the pageant with Kathie Lee Gifford, had turned away from the stage and was facing the television cameras.

I'd been nervous when I first met Regis backstage a few days before. He was talking too fast for me to understand him. I thought, "Oh, boy, here we go again!" Backstage I had to remind him three times to talk more slowly. But during our live interview on television, he spoke to me beautifully!

He had already announced that fourth runner-up was Tiffany Storm, Miss Indiana; third runner-up was Andrea Krahn, Miss Georgia; and second runner-up was Jennifer Makris, Miss New Jersey.

I was already mentally preparing to be first runner-up. I had learned that in the last ten years or so, contestants who won both the swimsuit and talent competitions became the favorites, only to consequently end the competition as first runner-up. That situation had happened to Teresa Strickland in 1978. And in an eerie coincidence, it was a Miss Virginia who won during Teresa's year, and yet here I was, holding Miss Virginia's hand!

Miss Virginia, Cullen Johnson, stood beside me. Regis wasn't facing me, so I couldn't read his lips. I heard a buzzing and saw the wave of applause in the audience. I heard him say, "Miss Virginia," but I missed the other words.

I didn't know if I'd won or not. I kept thinking, *If Miss Virginia cries, she won*, but when I turned to look at her, Cullen Johnson was pointing at me.

My mind went blank. I was overwhelmed, flooded with mixed emotions—words can't describe my feelings. *It's here.*

*You're here. This is not a dream, your reality is here. This is not a
daydream. This is real!*

I walked over to Kimberly Aiken, she pinned the crown to
my head. Someone handed me the Waterford crystal scepter. I
had no clue that I was even holding it until I found it in my
hand backstage. Pageant officials would have fainted if I had
dropped it! From the corner of my eye I saw Kathie Lee Gifford
applauding with tears in her eyes. Some automatic part of my
consciousness propelled me toward the crowd. *Turn. Wave.
Walk forward to the end of the runway. Turn again, walk back to
Kimberly.*

I finally pulled myself together as I walked down the runway. I stood for a moment at the far end, overwhelmed by the
cheering audience, and in my heart I cried out to God: *I really
need you, God. You'd better come with me now.*

I realized this job was going to be a huge responsibility. Yes,
I had found success, but with it would come more responsibility
than I had ever known. I remembered Colleen Kay Hutchins's
admonition to future Miss Americas, and I set my heart toward
becoming the best Miss America I could be.

I was twenty-one years old, and the only time I'd ever been
"employed" was a single baby-sitting job. This was not only a
pageant, it was a job, the biggest challenge I had ever faced.
And like the choice my parents made for me as a child, the
decisions I would make in the months to come would affect the
rest of my life.

I was the first deaf Miss America, the first, in fact, with any
type of physical disability. I knew everyone would look at me
as a pioneer of sorts, and I would represent over forty-eight
million Americans with some sort of disability. . . .

I suspected there would be a lot of pressure in the days
ahead, a relentless spotlight, and pressure from the media. I was
scared.

I looked for my family. At the beginning of the week, only my family waved the "I love you" sign, so it was easy to find them in the audience. But that night the sign had spread like a virus through the crowd. Almost everyone waved the "I love you" sign and I could not find my family.

3   The Whirlwind Begins

*I*mmediately after the telecast, I was escorted off the stage by a bevy of pageant officials. As I walked through the hallways backstage, Leanza Cornett, a former Miss America representing *Entertainment Tonight,* stopped me and asked for a comment. As the video camera honed in on my face, I smiled at Leanza and said, "I just can't believe it. I'll have to see the videotape to know it really happened!"

Right after that quick *ET* interview, a security guard and the pageant hostess, Marilyn Feehan, escorted me to a huge office backstage. The office had been used by the chairman of the hostess committee during the week-long competition, and now I was given a moment of quiet in a private room to freshen my makeup and catch my breath. I just stood there staring at the tiny mirror on the table. I lifted my hand and touched the crown on my head, still unable to believe it was really mine. Then I looked at myself in that mirror and said, "You're the first deaf Miss America." My stomach tightened as I considered the thought. I was the first Miss America with a disability. In the year ahead I'd be like a pioneer, navigating my way through situations and circumstances no other Miss America had ever explored. There was really no one to ask for advice.

Someone knocked on the door, then Leonard Horn, president and CEO of the Miss America Organization, entered the room with a wide smile on his face. "Congratulations, Heather," he said, and while I stammered my thanks, he leaned forward and kissed me on my forehead. I was so relieved! I wasn't certain how the national Miss America office would feel about a Miss America with a disability, but with that fatherly kiss Leonard Horn had demonstrated that they would be one hundred percent supportive. That kiss made my night, and I knew that for the next twelve months we would work together as a team.

"Heather?" Marilyn said, smiling at me. "Are you ready to meet the world?"

I took a deep breath. I had sought this, God had put me here. It was time to face reality. I followed Marilyn out of the trailer.

Still in my evening gown and crown, I entered the "winner's circle," a huge room in the convention hall used for pageant-related press conferences. More chairs had been added, and bright lights had been set up. As soon as we entered, cameras began to flash; the effect was blinding.

As Marilyn Feehan introduced me, a quick and disturbing thought raced through my brain: *If I make a mistake here, it will follow me throughout my entire year as Miss America. Whatever I do tonight is for keeps. Forever.*

I stepped to the lectern and began to answer the reporters' questions. The interview happened so fast that I don't remember much about it. I remember clearly that they asked how I felt about winning the title, and I said I was excited to follow in the distinguished footsteps of former Miss Americas. Then, without thinking, I told them to stop taking pictures because their camera flashes were so bright, I couldn't read the lips of the people talking to me.

I didn't mean to be so outspoken, the words just slipped out of my mouth. But instead of being offended, the photographers laughed and gave their cameras a rest . . . for a few moments.

A scant nine minutes later, I was whisked away from the reporters and taken to a private area for my first official portrait session. Again, I smiled as photographers shot seventy-five pictures in six minutes. There was an official portrait with my family, one with a cellular phone (sponsors of the pageant), and others with Kimberly Aiken, Miss America 1994; Marsha Fulsom, the former first lady of Alabama; and Yolande Betbeze, Miss America 1951, the first Miss America from Alabama.

When the pictures were done, I found my mother and hugged her. In many ways, this evening had been her victory as well as mine. Without her encouragement, support, and some hard decisions, I would never have been able to enter even the Shelby County Junior Miss Pageant, let alone made the huge step I had made this night.

Many of my other family members were scattered throughout the room, and I greeted as many of them as I could in about twenty minutes. But soon I was ushered on, and at 1:07 A.M. I met the other forty-nine contestants and their families at a party.

When I walked into this party, I was greeted by a sea of hands signing "I love you." Teresa Strickland was at this party, crying her eyes out, and my heart squeezed when I looked at her. I wanted so badly for her to experience what I'd enjoyed on this night. She had come so close as first runner-up in September 1978, and then she had freely volunteered her time, her energy, and her love to help me win Miss America. I wanted to take the crown from my head and put it on hers.

Bittersweet happiness flowed through me as I greeted my fellow contestants. Earlier, after I had walked down the runway and thanked God for the opportunity of being Miss America, I turned and saw the other forty-nine contestants applauding behind me. There were no words to describe my immense gratitude for their kindness, patience, and friendships. Honestly, there was not one among them who I'd consider a bad person. I treasure my special moments with Miss Ohio, Lea Mack; Miss South Carolina, Kristie Greene; Miss New Hampshire, Shannon Heather Hastings; Miss Hawaii, Courtney Glaza; Miss Alaska, Patricia Marlow; Miss Missouri, Ann Marie Sun; Miss Utah, Brooke Anderson; Miss Arkansas, Beth Anne Rankin; and Miss West Virginia, Jennifer Bopp.

But though I had overwhelmingly positive feelings about all of them, as I looked at them and began to walk back to the stage, suddenly the old sense of isolation crept back over me. I felt alone again, pulled apart. Everyone on that stage knew what it felt like to be a state winner, we all had that experience in common. They had all worked as hard as I did, but unfortunately only one young woman could be Miss America. At that moment I wished the rules could change so they could all be Miss America with me.

I smiled at them now. I honestly do not remember what I said to them, but I believe I thanked the contestants, my friends, fans of the Miss America Pageant, and my family for their support. I remember making the comment that Mickey Mouse had brought us all together—we contestants had spent the previous weekend together at Disney World, and that's where we became friends.

"I love you all," I told them before I was gently taken by the hand and led on to another party at Trump Plaza, this one given for pageant sponsors and judges. I mingled there for about half an hour, expressing my thanks to the many people who had made the night possible.

At this party I recognized a little deaf girl I'd met earlier during pageant week. During the "parade of the states" in Atlantic City, I had seen this little girl standing by the side of the road with a poster in her hands. The poster said HI, HEATHER, I'M DEAF TOO, and she had drawn a picture of a hand positioned in the "I love you" sign. Someone had found her and brought her to the sponsor's party. She was so tired, but I hugged her and thanked her mother for bringing her to the party. She was the first of many deaf children I would meet as Miss America.

It was nearly two A.M. when we returned to Harrahs, my hotel, and I was surprised to find that all my things had been moved to the Presidential Suite. There were roses everywhere, in the bedroom, the living room, even in the bathroom, where a huge whirlpool bath looked inviting. My family waited there to greet me: my mom, my dad and his wife, Terri; Melissa and her husband Tony; Uncle Bruce; Aunt Gloria; Aunt Deborah; Aunt Stephanie; Uncle Jimmy and his wife, Debra; Granddaddy and Grandmother Gray; Stacey and her baby daughter, Tessa; and my cousins Erika, Christopher, Holly, Trey, Ben, and Matthew.

After hugging my family, I looked around the gorgeous suite, oohed and ahhed over the bedroom, and thanked the security men for watching over me. My family stayed for about an hour, then everyone but Mother left. We stood in the bedroom, alone together for the first time since I'd become Miss America. I was excited, telling Mother about how I had received a telegram from Sandi Patty saying that she was planning to watch the pageant that night. I went on talking about all the people who had sent me cards and messages with good wishes, and then Mother suddenly said, "Heather, the strangest thing happened to me tonight. You know how I'm always such a nervous wreck before your pageants?"

Of course I did. We'd been through so many together.

"Well," she went on, "tonight I wasn't the least bit nervous. Just before we went on the air, this strange warmth washed over me. And then it was as if I heard a voice saying, 'Relax and enjoy. Tonight is hers!' "

I felt the hair lift on my arms. That was so strange! Slowly, I nodded and then told her a similar thing had happened to me. "Just before the pageant started tonight, I was standing backstage, when a strange warmth passed through my body too. And I heard a voice say, 'Relax and dance for me tonight.' And I wasn't nervous at all!"

Mother and I looked at each other in silent awe, both of us struck speechless by the presence and awareness of God. I could feel his warmth in my heart. And I knew he was real.

Finally I was left alone in that magnificent suite. I knew I ought to be trying to catch every single moment of sleep, but I was still as excited as a child at Christmas. I sat on the bed and looked around, then suddenly felt a headache coming on. My temples were beginning to pound, and I couldn't figure out why I'd have a headache now, when I was finally finished with tension! I lifted my hand to my pounding head, and then felt the cool metal and glass crown beneath my hand.

I took the crown off, then put it on the table and took a long, hard look at it. It wasn't unusually heavy, but it was more weight than my head was used to bearing. Was it possible that wearing the crown might bring pain as well as pleasure?

I hoped a good night's sleep would chase the headache away. After slipping out of my evening gown and putting on pajamas, I climbed into that big bed and stared at the crown again. As a child I'd fallen asleep dreaming of dancing, but on that night I fell asleep looking at the rhinestones that gleamed in the slight light from a lamp in the living room.

The First Morning

I woke up at eight the next morning. When I looked in the mirror, I noticed that my eyes were red and huge. My body felt exhausted, but my heart was ready to go. I couldn't wait to begin my first full day as Miss America.

A nine o'clock media briefing was followed by a ten o'clock press conference. At ten-thirty I went outside and had photos taken with my new car—a Chevrolet Camaro convertible. I had never owned my own car, and at home had driven my family's boxy station wagon and a tanklike Oldsmobile. I couldn't believe that my first car was not only gorgeous, it was free!

At eleven I had to change into shorts and a T-shirt for the traditional beach photos—I forgot to bring tennis shoes, so I had to wear the black high heels I'd worn with my suit that morning! At noon we shot more photos for Chevrolet. Huge crowds gathered everywhere I went, and I felt a little awkward during the photo shoots. I'd never been a model (at five four, I'm definitely not the model type), yet here I was with everyone watching while cameras flashed. Worse yet, I couldn't read the photographer's lips when they covered their faces with their cameras, so they'd have to give me instructions, then step back, focus, and shoot. I'm afraid I may have frustrated them, but they accepted the unexpected difficulty with good grace.

At one-thirty we hurried back to the hotel to pack and move out. I hadn't even spent twelve hours in my luxurious suite before it was time to go.

During the two-hour limousine ride from Atlantic City to New York City, I had my first opportunity to sit and think. For the past three years I had been preparing and concentrating on being the best I could be, but suddenly, overnight, everything had changed. I no longer had to worry about looking good in an evening gown and swimsuit, I no longer had to practice my ballet every day.

The future suddenly seemed uncertain and a little frightening. I looked out the window, hoping to find some sign or assurance from God, but I could see no answers. I'd have to wait, to be patient . . . old lessons I thought I had learned in ballet class.

I knew that if I weren't deaf I could rely on the experience of the Miss Americas who'd gone before me, but not one of them had faced the world with a disability. I wondered what would happen in the months ahead, and then I remembered that I could . . . and must . . . trust God completely.

Sitting in the limo with my two Miss America traveling companions, I silently set a goal for myself: *This will be the best year of my life.*

In the week that followed, I became well acquainted with the two women who would be traveling with me throughout my term of service as Miss America. Bonnie Sirgany and Michelle (Mickey) Brennan were both with me during those first tumultuous days, but after my initial baptism into the Miss America routine they traveled with me on alternate months. Later in the year, Bonnie showed me a peculiar collection of photographs. She had taken pictures of several Miss Americas asleep in the car.

"When did you take these?" I asked, looking at the photos.

"The day after each of them won," she explained. "But I couldn't take a picture of you, Heather. You were the only Miss America I know who didn't take a nap in the car."

In my first breathless forty-eight hours as Miss America I appeared on the NBC *Today* show, *Live with Regis and Kathie Lee*, and *The Tonight Show with Jay Leno*. I also met with sponsors of the Miss America Pageant and reporters who wanted to write personality profiles for their newspapers or magazines.

My first official interview as Miss America took place on *The Today Show* with Bryant Gumbel. Normally Katie Couric interviewed Miss America every year, but she was not there that day. Bryant was very nice and tried his best to communicate. It was a little difficult for me to understand him, but he asked the same questions most reporters ask: "How do you hear the music? How do you feel about being Miss America?" And "What are you going to do during your Miss America year?"

I was excited to see Regis and Kathie Lee again. Being interviewed on *Live with Regis and Kathie Lee* was almost like visiting old friends. I waited backstage for nearly an hour and met Melissa Gilbert, who I'd known from her role on *Little House on the Prairie*. Actress Emma Samms was also backstage, and not only was she famous for her roles on *General Hospital* and *Dynasty*, she had been one of the judges at the Miss America Pageant.

Emma was so sweet. Her eyes sparkled with joy as she came up to me. "Heather, we judges were not supposed to talk to each other until after the pageant was over," she said. "But after Regis announced you as the winner, we had a chance to talk. Every one of us wanted you to win. We were so excited for you!" She lowered her voice to a more personal tone. "I loved your dance. I took ballet classes when I was younger and I always dreamed of becoming a prima ballerina, but a hip injury prevented me from reaching my dream."

I knew how disappointed she must have felt. Even though I had never been injured, by then I was too old to join a nationally known ballet company.

I really appreciated Emma's generous support. Later she would invite me to appear at a function for the Starlight Foundation, an international organization she cofounded to help seriously ill children and their families.

Kathie Lee and Regis greeted me warmly when I stepped

out of the Green Room to meet them. Regis's eyes were sparkling, and he seemed more relaxed than he had during the Miss America Pageant. He opened the wooden box containing my crown and held it up to show the audience. I felt a unique bond between Kathie Lee and myself. At the time I wasn't sure why I felt this closeness, but later I learned that she has Jesus in her heart. She understood my heart perfectly.

As I talked about my STARS program during our interview, Kathie Lee began to cry. I didn't know what to do, but kept talking and just looked at Regis. Kathie Lee got off her chair and stepped away to find a box of tissues. I stopped talking, amazed as she walked around giving tissues to people in the audience. Then she came back to us and handed me a tissue. "Oh, no," I said, laughing. "I don't need it. I'm fine."

The audience was laughing too. Kathie Lee and Regis were a lot of fun. I really loved working with them.

Immediately after my interview with Kathie Lee and Regis, I flew to Las Vegas, Nevada, to tape *The Tonight Show with Jay Leno*. The show usually tapes in Los Angeles, but Las Vegas was serving as a special guest city for the show that week.

Soon after arriving in the guest waiting room with my traveling companion, I heard a knock on the door. When I answered it, Jay was standing there in blue jeans and a casual shirt. It took me a full thirty seconds to recognize him, then I realized *Jay Leno* was standing in front of me.

As usual, I said the first thought that buzzed through my brain. "What are *you* doing here?"

"I'm here to talk to you about what we're going to do tonight on the show."

Stunned, I let him in. I felt a little strange, treating a celebrity like a real person, but he was humble and thoughtful as we talked. I thought he might make fun of me on the show, so I was a little nervous. But as we prepared for the interview, he said, "Heather, I want you to know that I really appreciate your parents. It's obvious that they never felt sorry for you, and they treated you like any normal child. I liked hearing about the time when you were watching TV and your mother was calling your name. You heard her and turned toward her, but then turned back to the TV."

"I know," I said, laughing. "I was being naughty. I told her I couldn't hear her because the battery of my hearing aid was nearly dead."

"But she didn't take your excuse seriously," Jay answered. "And I think it's important to let parents know that no matter what happens to their children, those children have the same heart we all have. They need to be treated just like any other kid."

I was surprised when he told me that, but developed an instant respect for him. We told that story on the air, and the audience seemed to love it.

The Winds of Criticism

I had thought that Miss America was America's sweetheart, but I quickly found out that nothing could be further from the truth. Most people are kind and gracious, but there are others who are quick to find fault. Almost immediately after winning the pageant, I became aware of criticism from some deaf people. They were upset because I spoke instead of signing during the pageant.

The door opened on all those memories I'd tried to bury—my feelings of worthlessness and failure at the Miss Deaf Alabama pageant, my conviction that I would never find a place to fit in. I had worked *so hard* to speak, it had taken me six years to pronounce my last name correctly, my family and I had sacrificed so much in order that I might stand on a stage and *speak* my name instead of signing it. And out of eighty thousand women who compete on various levels each year for the Miss America crown, I'd been successful. And yet there were those who felt it their duty to stand back and criticize.

The situation worsened when the media caught wind of the criticism. It seems that no one is as interested in hearing good things as they are in hearing bad, and so the press immediately jumped on the supposed "clash" between the new deaf Miss America and the deaf community.

After that first cloud of controversy appeared, I suffered from nightmares for a week. I dreamed hideous, dark dreams in which photographers lay in wait everywhere, hiding behind curtains, behind chairs, in bushes, waiting to snap a picture of me.

I was beginning to think that my bright hopes of influencing the deaf community would vanish like morning mist. I heard feedback that led me to believe that the deaf culture didn't appreciate my hard work. I felt that some deaf people looked at me as a sort of freak. I knew I wasn't a monster. I was willing to lend my voice to help them, but they didn't seem to care. No matter how hard I tried to talk about my platform and the STARS program, some deaf people always managed to bring up the controversy about speaking versus signing.

I didn't know what to do. I wanted to help, but no matter how hard I tried to bring hope, I seemed to do damage instead. I thought maybe everyone would be better off if I just resigned my title. I was twenty-one years old, and I had led a fairly sheltered life. I didn't have anyone to turn to except God. So I poured out my heart to him and gave the responsibility of my new job . . . and his dream for me . . . back to God. I prayed for strength, and for someone to guide me through the controversies that still lay ahead.

God was faithful and answered my prayer. He reminded me that he allowed trials in my life for his reasons, and he wanted me to learn to depend upon him completely. It was as if he said, "Heather, you can quit and depend on yourself, or you can rest on me. I'm in charge, and everything is happening for a good reason."

I decided to follow God. I'm glad I made that choice, because it enabled me to handle difficult situations gracefully instead of with anger and bitterness. I heard the criticism, but I continued to offer a positive message and mention helpful ideas that could help those in the deaf culture to climb the ladder of career success. I ended my speeches by saying, "Although not everyone feels my STARS program works for them, I hope they can find some benefit from my advice and example. I have had tremendous support from people who have disabilities. They were very excited by my becoming Miss America. They say, 'You help people who don't have disabilities change their perspective. You tell everyone that we are people first. Our disability comes second.'"

In answering my prayer for guidance, God led me to Washington, D.C., where I met Donna Dickman and John Healy.

I had met John Healy during my first week of service as Miss America. He owned a public relations firm in Chicago, Prescott Healy Company, Ltd., which has served as the primary public relations consultant for the Miss America Organization for several years. John really impressed me with his strong Christian commitment. He encouraged me to think about God's will before making decisions about how to address disabilities issues.

John once presented me with a very lovely pen. "You are a national spokeswoman now," he said after giving me the gift. "Your opinions can influence people and make them think twice about people with disabilities."

"Come on, John," I said, blushing. "No one really takes me

seriously. I'm just Miss America. It's not like I'm the First Lady or anything."

"No, Heather." His gaze was serious. "You have a strong voice now. You can speak about disabilities issues and people will listen. They are interested in you."

His attitude caught me off guard. My STARS program was a motivational speech, not a serious treatise on disabilities. Now, as a public figure, I found myself being asked questions for which I was unprepared. Other Miss Americas had been able to stick to discussing their platforms, but I had become an unexpected ambassador for people with disabilities—nearly fifty million of them.

Entering Politics

From out of the blue I was invited to join the President's Committee on the Employment of People with Disabilities. Tony Coelho, the committee chairman, invited me to join the committee whose purpose was "to involve key representatives from the business, disability, and service communities, with the support of the President of the United States, in a national effort designed to further employment opportunities for people with disabilities."

I was greatly honored by the invitation, and decided to keep quiet about the fact that I'm a staunch Republican, not a Democrat. I accepted because I didn't want to hurt the reputation of the Miss America Organization, and I sincerely hoped to be able to make a difference in people's lives. I thought I could help to tear barriers down even though I didn't agree with some of the President's philosophies.

At my first meeting with the President's committee, I met

Dr. Donna Dickman, executive director of the Alexander Graham Bell Association for the Deaf. I knew right away that Donna was a very positive person. Some of the people who had been invited to meet and share information with me were quite firm about letting me know that my positive "anything is possible" platform wasn't realistic. They pointed out that they'd been fighting for equal rights in the workplace for years. Others shared sad stories and summarized their positions by saying that life simply wasn't fair.

I was beginning to notice that some people with disabilities have negative attitudes. They always see the glass as half empty instead of half full. I can understand why they'd be unhappy if they find it difficult to get a job, but that unhappiness will hurt their prospects for employment. I know how it feels to be discriminated against, but there is always hope.

After I attended JSU for two years, I transferred to a different college that offered a great accounting program. Because I couldn't read the instructors' lips, I went to the office of student services and asked if either a sign language interpreter or a computer typist could be provided for my classes. "Of course not, we can't spoon-feed you," I was told.

Spoon-feed? Sometimes I felt like some *hearing* students were the ones being spoon-fed! Having an interpreter or someone to type the instructor's words certainly wouldn't pamper me, it would only help me stand on level ground with my classmates. I wanted to be an independent student. Having an interpreter would have helped me reach that goal, but they couldn't see from my perspective.

So I can understand frustration, even anger. But I didn't give up when I was turned down. I kept going until I found a workable solution, and I worked double time to keep up with everyone else. And through it all, I tried to look for the positive things in my life, not the "I can'ts" but the "I cans."

I was particularly inspired by Eddie Espinosa, special assistant to the chairman of the President's Committee on Employment of People with Disabilities. Eddie often deals with people's complaints, but though he has a difficult job and is confined to a wheelchair, I never once saw him lose his smile or his gentle spirit. I loved being around him.

I was disturbed by the negative attitudes I saw and heard in those committee meetings. "They don't see the golden opportunities that surround them every day!" I ranted, waving my hands as I talked to Eddie on the phone. "I want people to open their hearts to the possibilities of success, but they keep looking at the past, they just won't change!"

Eddie, as calm as always, said, "Heather, I know it's hard. But you've got to trust me. It may take time, but you will make a difference."

After that first meeting of the President's committee, I was beginning to think I'd made a mistake by joining, but Donna Dickman grinned at me with a smile that said she believed in me. "I was so excited when you won this golden opportunity to serve America," she told me privately. "The night you were crowned Miss America, your dream was realized and my dream was born." She went on to explain that she wanted to give me the honor of recognizing the achievement of deaf students across the nation. Because it was the seventy-fifth anniversary of the Miss America Pageant, the Alexander Graham Bell Association for the Deaf would find seventy-five noteworthy deaf students. Each of the seventy-five STARS students would receive a $1,000 savings bond and a special STARS recognition award.

I felt my heart turn over in delight. I knew this woman would be part of my support team for life. I could not find the words to describe my gratitude for her vision and her unbelievable faith in me.

Washington, D.C.

Shortly after winning the crown, I had lunch in Washington with the congressional delegates from Alabama, among them Senator Richard Shelby, Senator Howell Heflin, and Representative Spencer Bachus. From the Capitol building, the delegates helped me launch my STARS program in a press conference that included reporters from CNN, *USA Today*, and all the major networks. I was asked to give a short speech, and when I'd finished, Senator Heflin (who lives in Tuscumbia, Alabama, where Helen Keller lived) stepped forward and proclaimed that I was the second Helen Keller. Though I was a bit taken aback to be compared to the woman I'd always idolized, I appreciated his sincerity.

One of the people who impressed me most in Washington was Senator Bob Dole. He was a real gentleman, and he has a disability too—due to a combat injury from World War II, he has little use of his right arm. While some people seemed to treat their meeting with me as a "duty" or a "photo op," he looked into my eyes as we talked, and behaved as though no one in the room was more important than I. Unlike most politicians I met, he actually listened more than he spoke. I noticed his remarkably humble attitude and decided to emulate it as best I could.

Through Senator Dole's example on that first day I met him, I realized that I had only one chance to meet people for the first time, and people remember that first impression forever. I made a note to try my best to be positive every day. That's tough when you're in the spotlight of celebrity. Even after only a few weeks of wearing the Miss America crown, I'd come to realize that truth.

During the 1996 election, my husband and I were privileged to travel with Bob and Elizabeth Dole throughout the last several days of that hectic, exhausting campaign. During this time I saw that Senator Dole was more than the typical politician. He was a perfect embodiment of my STARS platform. He was an incredibly positive person. I saw him stand up and give his best in a speech when I knew he was tired and not feeling well. I watched how he worked hard as he struggled to achieve his dream of becoming president. And then I saw him and his wife graciously accept the will of the American people as they voted to elect the incumbent, Bill Clinton.

My husband and I were pleased and proud to be a small part of Bob Dole's support team. In years to come, I know I will tell my children that Bob Dole, and men like him, are true American heroes. They follow their dreams and learn from the journey, even when that journey seems to end in defeat.

I will never think of Bob Dole as defeated. He is a true patriot. And I will always remember when he gave his acceptance speech in San Diego and told the world, "I stand here as a man at the mercy of God." Senator Dole is not ashamed to tell the world that whatever happens, he is willing to follow God's plan for his life.

Even though I don't agree with all the policies of the Clinton administration, I did enjoy meeting Hillary and the President at the White House. During my ten-minute meeting with Mrs. Clinton, I found that Hillary and I actually had two things in common: controversy and media attention.

"Stand up for your beliefs," the First Lady told me. "Be true to yourself. I have the same problem you do."

She was then gracious enough to escort me to meet her husband. Hillary walked me through a crowd of waiting people in the lobby, then led me into the Oval Office. I could feel the power of the place when I walked into the room. A gorgeous rug emblazoned with an eagle covered the floor, and a big window behind the President's desk flooded the room with light.

Mrs. Clinton led me to her husband and said, "This is my husband, Bill Clinton. Mr. President, I'd like you to meet Heather Whitestone, Miss America."

I smiled, careful to show the respect the president's office deserves. I thanked President Clinton for his support of people with disabilities, then we made small talk for a moment while he showed me his desk, one that had belonged to John F. Kennedy. Like a giddy girl, I blurted out, "Wow! My dad and grandparents own an Ethan Allen furniture store, and this desk is much better than the desks of Ethan Allen!"

Bill Clinton laughed. Then, as suddenly as if a bell had rung, the press secretary opened a door and the press streamed in to take pictures. While they snapped and flashed, I tried to smile naturally.

Heather, take a deep breath. Look. You're standing in the most powerful office in the world, beside the President, right in front of Kennedy's desk. Who are you, Heather? Why should you be here?

I didn't know. I didn't feel ready. I could barely accept where and what and who I was. The girl who'd had only a few friends, whom few people had ever taken seriously, was standing in the Oval Office next to the President while a horde of photographers scrambled to take pictures.

I wasn't the only one who wondered why I'd been chosen. I spoke often to children as representatives of different pageants, and at one elementary school where I was speaking as Miss Cullman, a little guy stood, scrunched up his face, and said, "Just because you're handicapped doesn't mean you're better than anyone else, you know."

A couple of teachers moved to shush him, but I stopped them. "No, he can say anything he wants," I said, bending to look him in the eye. "And you're right, young man. You should look at people first, not at their disability. But I didn't win the pageant because I was deaf. I won it because I worked hard."

The Dream Evolves

As I began to adjust to the reality of being the first Miss America with a disability, I realized that my dream had changed. Now that I possessed the crown and title I'd sought, I had a new goal. Like Helen Keller, who used her powerful voice to bring hope to people with disabilities, I wanted to bring that same hope and light to the world. I thought that perhaps the way to achieve my goals might be through political office, but it didn't take long for me to lose patience with the system in Washington. Some wonderful people are involved in government, but politics seemed to be more a system of trading favors than the serious business of improving people's lives. And everywhere I turned, eager to shine my light, I met with controversy and criticism.

My first appearance for a deaf community took place at the Memphis Oral School in Memphis, Tennessee. That appearance was a mixed blessing. Even though I really wanted to make an impact on deaf students, the students in this gathering were only five years old, little more than babies. But there I met Lynda Mead, Miss America 1960. She was warm and charming, and regularly volunteered to work with this school for the deaf.

Though I loved meeting Lynda and being with the children, I still felt uncomfortable at that school because of the opposition I'd received from some deaf people. Three years before, when I had just begun to imagine myself as a bridge between the hearing and deaf worlds, I had been naïve and simplistic. Now that I was older and more seasoned in the ways of the world, I felt the tension between the deaf culture and the oral deaf world, and I didn't want to put myself in the middle of that conflict. I was in the public eye, and I didn't want to be a target—who would?

But then I found encouragement from a very unlikely source. King Jordan, president of Gallaudet University, the bastion of deaf culture in this country, wrote me a personal letter explaining a published article in which some Gallaudet students had been critical of my favoring speech over signing.

I was terribly impressed, even awed, that he would take the time to write. I knew he was deaf too. If I was finding it difficult to walk the line between the deaf and hearing worlds, how, I wondered, did he cope? He presided over a university for deaf students, and yet he had to offer them the choice of a future in the deaf or the hearing worlds.

King Jordan's note put things into perspective for me. Yes, some members of the media had been relentless in reporting every twitter or controversy and criticism. No, some deaf people did not fully understand my attitude, my motives, or my positions. But being Miss America wasn't the toughest job in the world. And God had promised to go on this journey with me.

I constantly had to remind myself to maintain a positive attitude. In his book, *Easy Doesn't Do It*, Derric Johnson talks about people who forget that Babe Ruth hit 714 home runs in his career and remember only that he struck out twice that often. And did you know that fishermen don't put tops on crab baskets? If one captured crab starts to climb up the side of the basket, the other crabs will reach up and pull it back down.[1]

There were days when I felt like one of those trapped crabs. Why are some people so quick to dwell on negative things? Though I am as human as anyone else, I don't want to dwell on life's miseries. I want to look for the bright, the right, the positive things. But as I traveled and spent more time with people with negative attitudes, I was distracted from looking

---

[1] *Easy Doesn't Do It*, p. 40.

for the positive and my dream slowly shriveled and died. I had great ambitions, but I learned that even Miss America can't change people's hearts unless they are willing to be changed. I received letters from mothers whose deaf children were encouraged and empowered by my success, but their hearts were young and optimistic. Those who were world-weary looked at my twenty-one-year-old face under that sparkling crown and pronounced me young and idealistic.

One bright moment in the early part of my reign came when Marlee Matlin, the first deaf actress to win an Oscar, told the deaf community that she respected my choice to speak and not sign. I was surprised and very grateful. I felt that God had brought her into my life to add encouragement, and I appreciated her risking censure to tell the deaf community to support me. She had a bouquet of red roses sent to my hotel when I first arrived in New York on my second day as Miss America. I will always be grateful for her support.

My confrontations with the disabilities lobby forced me to educate myself about the issues. I was appalled to learn that more than fifty percent of people with disabilities were unemployed at that time. When I met business people and asked how they felt about the Americans with Disabilities Act, I found that they would rather not talk about it. It is difficult for small companies to provide interpreters, special access, etc., for employees with disabilities. We need creative solutions to very real problems, and we still have a long way to go before disabilities are not a stumbling block to employment.

Fortunately, there were many kind souls who refreshed my spirit and added color to my life during those early weeks. One of the corporate sponsors for the Miss America Pageant was Den-Mat Corporation, the company that makes Rembrandt toothpaste. I met Dr. Robert L. Ibsen, the company president, and he completely changed my thinking about corporate America.

I had always thought of corporate heads as snobby, cigar-smoking types who wore rich suits and sat behind big desks all day, but Dr. Ibsen was so humble. When my traveling companion and I met him, he invited us to his house. I was expecting a majestic four-story home surrounded by a hundred manicured acres, and I was shocked when we arrived at his pleasant but ordinary home. He lived in the same house his family had purchased long before he became a corporate CEO. And his family was just like my family—natural and down-to-earth.

Dr. Ibsen was also very strong Christian, and his stand for Christ made a big impact on me. He reinforced my belief that true Christians don't change when they encounter success or wealth or fame. When you have Jesus in your heart, if you keep your eyes focused on him, you will grow to be like him. Money, success, and the things of the material world won't change the heart of a true believer whose eyes are focused on Christ.

I felt another touch of grace when I appeared on *The 700 Club* and met host Terry Meeuwsen, Miss America 1973. I really enjoyed this particular interview, because I had so few opportunities to talk openly about God. Most of my appearances were for businesses or schools or pageant sponsors, and I looked forward to sharing the story of how God had directed my path to this particular place.

I felt an instant rapport when I met Terry. She understood how tired I was, since she knew firsthand how great the demands of the title were and how strenuous life on the road could be. I had heard that she became so exhausted during her term of service that she had to spend two weeks in the hospital!

I was beginning to feel really tired, but Christmas vacation was looming bright on my calendar. I looked forward to going home, being with my family, and setting aside the Miss America crown . . . if only for a little while.

4 Breaking the Sound Barrier

*A*s dawn spread a gray light over my hotel room, I glanced over at the clock on the nightstand, knowing I had to get up early. The Macy's Thanksgiving Day parade was my scheduled assignment for the day, and though I knew I'd miss being around the holiday table with my family, the parade promised to be fun. I was to ride a float with children dressed in international costumes, and they would join me in signing the song, "Love in Any Language." I knew there'd be lines of expectant children along the parade route, and I didn't want to disappoint them. Their smiles would enrich my life.

By November I was accustomed to the 20,000-miles-a-month schedule and the endless succession of hotels. My steadfast "be sweet to those who criticize" policy had begun to reap benefits. The criticism wasn't going to go away, but it takes two to have an argument. I learned that if I didn't respond to those who attacked me, the press had very little to report.

I was *so* ready to go home for Christmas. I'd developed a

whole new appreciation for the simple things I'd always taken for granted. Everywhere we went I had to take along three huge suitcases, and I was always embarrassed to explain to the bellmen that I had to pack all kinds of clothes because I never knew what climate I'd be in. The poor bellmen were sweating under the load of my heavy luggage, and but I'd explain that I had to be prepared for anything. I often joked with people that it would be so much easier if Miss America had a uniform. That would save her from countless headaches, and spare the backs of a thousand bellmen!

I wanted to slide those suitcases into a closet and forget about traveling for a few days. I imagined that my time at home would be restful, relaxed, and refreshing. I wanted to put the crown away in its little wooden box, spend hours washing clothes (oh, how I came to appreciate the advantages of a washer and dryer!), and just sit around with my hair down and no makeup on. I hate to sound ungracious, but after four months of repeatedly being asked the same questions, signing autographs, and smiling at photographers, I was ready for a complete change of pace.

But unfortunately Christmas didn't offer that change, and actually turned out to be anything *but* restful. The good people of Birmingham looked at me as a hometown girl; they felt I belonged to them. And also, my family *knew* I belonged to *them*. So instead of a change in routine on my vacation, I found myself fielding the same old questions: "Heather, tell us about all the people you've met." "Tell us where you've been." "What's Kathie Lee really like?" "What have you been doing in the last few weeks?"

I couldn't very well tell people to leave me alone. When they started in with the old familiar questions, I'm afraid my eyes would glaze over. I didn't want to talk about Miss America. I really didn't want to autograph a hundred pictures. All I wanted—all I *needed*—was sleep and rest. Everyone I met wanted the inside scoop on everything, but at that point I couldn't think of any fascinating stories about what I'd been doing; all I could remember of my year was an endless series of fancy dinners, airplane cabins, and slips of paper outstretched for an autograph.

I was home for two weeks, but that wasn't long enough to get any real rest. Shortly after the beginning of the new year, I was back to work. My calendar had filled with a lot of fun activities during the post-holiday season. In addition to the Macy's parade, I was scheduled to ride floats in the Rose and Orange Bowl parades too.

On New Year's Eve in Miami, after I'd just ridden in the Orange Bowl parade, Mickey and I made plans to go watch the "orange" rise up to the top of the hotel at the stroke of midnight. (Times Square in New York has its apple, Miami has an orange!) I was too tired to entertain people, so I suggested to Mickey that we go out in casual clothes. I washed the makeup off my face and left my hair down. I slipped into blue jeans, a T-shirt, and tennis shoes. Dressed "down," Mickey and I walked outside to the park in front of the hotel and found two seats in the crowd that had gathered to watch. I felt my heart turn over with happiness. Here I was, lost in the crowd, and no one knew who I was. I had my old life back!

A commotion caused a disturbance about twenty feet away, and I looked over to see Megan Welch, Miss Florida, who had competed with me in Atlantic City. Surrounded by security guards and traveling companions, she wore a business suit with a sparkling rhinestone tiara brooch. Lots of people in the waiting crowd, still counting the minutes until midnight, decided to kill time by asking for her autograph.

I felt a stab of guilt. I really should have gone over to say hello, but if I did, Megan would acknowledge me, and I did not want to spend any more time facing the public. I turned to Mickey: "I really feed bad about not saying hello to her, but I don't want to deal with autographs now."

"Don't worry," Mickey whispered back. "You need to have a good time. This is your break."

About ten minutes later, a family seated near us recognized me. They were excited and asked for my signature, but I made a little deal with them first. If they wouldn't say a word to anyone else, I'd give them an autograph. They agreed, so I signed their papers and then spent the rest of 1994 talking to them and enjoying their company. I really appreciated them for allowing me to have one special night as "one of the crowd."

I had been thrilled to receive two very special invitations from one very dear lady: Kathie Lee Gifford. After meeting me in Atlantic City at the pageant, she had invited me to dance for her televised Christmas special, and sign the national anthem as she sang at the Super Bowl in January.

I had always admired Kathie Lee. She had more jobs than I, and yet she always seemed to do a good job of staying on top of things. She not only woke before the sun every morning to host *Live with Regis and Kathie Lee*, she was a devoted mother of two young children. She made commercials for Carnival Cruise Lines and frequent public appearances. She planned her Christmas special, wrote books, and oversaw a clothing line for Wal-Mart. She was also a strong and outspoken Christian.

I was delighted to dance to "Do You Hear What I Hear?" on her Christmas TV special. While we were preparing the dance steps a month or so before the taping, a famous dance teacher from New York came into the rehearsal studio and asked me to play the role of a homeless mother who teaches her children how to fight with a group of "invaders" who wanted to take over her territory. The idea of teaching children to fight disturbed me, and I told the dance teacher that we did not donated airtime amounted to nearly one million dollars. In addition, NBC agreed to air a separate PSA on early detection as part of its "The More You Know" campaign during network prime time. Natus Medical, Incorporated, underwrote thirty-second and sixty-second radio announcements, which were distributed to over 6,000 stations and received over 7,350 air plays, reaching over fifty million listeners in forty-three states.

Another one thousand billboards were donated by the Outdoor Advertising Association of America to the early identification campaign, a contribution of more than one million dollars in free advertising space, creative design, poster production, and fees. The billboards, which featured an infant and his mother interacting with me beside the headline "Listen to Miss America," was designed and donated by Nancy van Daal-Klaud of 3M Media in Bedford Park, Illinois.

Finally, newspaper stories about my involvement with the early identification program were distributed to 1,200 suburban and weekly newspapers, including 200 Spanish-language papers. These stories reached nearly 1,585,000 readers.

Donna Dickman later told me that this campaign resulted in over 4,000 calls to the Bell Association for specific information about early identification of hearing loss. I sincerely hope that many more families contacted their physician for the immediate testing of their little ones.

Seventy-five Shining Stars

Without the Alexander Graham Bell Association for the Deaf, I know I would not have made nearly the positive difference I was able to attempt during my term of service. Along with the early identification of hearing loss campaign, the AG Bell Association kicked off the "75 Stars" program that was Donna

need to bring another tragic story to the world, especially at Christmastime.

The teacher walked out without even saying good-bye. I was shocked at the abrupt dismissal, but I did not regret either my decision or what I had said. We hear enough about tragedy on the news—why invent more for Christmas?

I was happy to return my attention to the hope-filled "Do You Hear What I Hear?" I asked if it would be okay for Monica Smith, my dance teacher, to help us with the dance, and Kathie Lee not only invited Monica to New York, but also brought several of Monica's bright young students to perform with me. Monica did a wonderful job, especially since she had only two weeks to work with the young girls. The resulting dance was beautifully designed and danced, and Monica made my job so much easier. Once again, I don't know what I would have done without her.

I'll never forget the time Kathie Lee and I were together at the Super Bowl. I was feeling a little frazzled from constantly moving to a different city every sixteen to thirty-six hours. Kathie Lee came into the room where we were to wait until it was time to perform "The Star-Spangled Banner." She sat down, propped her arms on the chair, then looked me in the eye and asked, "Heather, are you exhausted?"

"Yes." I couldn't help grinning. She was tired too; I could see it in her eyes, and yet I knew in just a few moments she'd be standing before a crowd of thousands and putting her entire heart into a very difficult song.

"Let me share something with you," she said, closing her eyes. "There's a Bible verse I always remember when I'm feeling tired."

And then she shared the verse with me. I don't remember exactly which one it was, but it had something to do with praising the Lord. I was so thrilled to hear her quote the word of God. I had met many celebrities by that time, and not one other person had ever thought to share a verse of Scripture with me. Kathie Lee had also shared the good news about Jesus on her televised Christmas special. I don't think she knew it then, but her example really challenged me.

Early Identification of Hearing Loss

Not long after the new year, God brought me a new and unexpected dream: the early identification of hearing loss program. The program was the brain child of my friend Donna Dickman, Ph.D., executive director of the Alexander Graham Bell Association for the Deaf.

Early detection of hearing loss is important because the vast majority of deaf children are born to hearing parents. Hearing impairment is the most common disability in newborns, affecting one in every two hundred babies in the United States— more than 70,000 babies per year. Nevertheless, the average child's age when deafness is detected is thirty months, and by that age the most critical period for development of speech and language skills has nearly passed.

I was fortunate that my mother dropped that stack of pans when I was twenty-one months old. The longer an impairment goes undetected, the more severe the outcome.

Despite the experts' encouragement to screen early for hearing loss, only about ten to fifteen percent of babies are tested before they are three months old. We need to do better. Only about six hundred hospitals in the United States routinely screen newborn infants for hearing loss before the babies go home from the hospital, although the screening techniques are simple, reliable, and relatively inexpensive. If hearing loss is not identified in the nursery, there is often a delay of up to a

year between the parent's initial concern and the actual diagnosis of hearing loss. All too often when the parent expresses concern to the physician, the child is not immediately referred for hearing testing. My advice to parents who are concerned about the possibility of hearing loss in their child is that they insist that the child be tested. No child is too young for a hearing test. The technology is readily available, but parents have to be persistent.

Early detection screening will benefit all of us. According to those who have examined the economic impact of hearing loss, an estimated $23.4 billion is spent each year on programs and services for individuals with communicative disabilities. Those costs include special education, vocational rehabilitation, hearing aids, speech pathology, and personnel training. Furthermore, more than four billion dollars is lost to society because the average income of individuals who are deaf is less than that of hearing people.

In March 1995 Donna Dickman and I launched what was the nation's largest public service campaign aimed at early identification of hearing loss. At a luncheon held at the National Press Club, we explained that the Alexander Graham Bell Association for the Deaf, together with the Miss America Organization, would utilize television, radio, print, and outdoor media to encourage parents to have their children tested. An 800 number featured on billboards and print media would make it easy for parents to request a free hearing checklist to recognize any hearing loss in their young children.

Donna and I were thrilled that so many people enthusiastically joined in the campaign. We filmed a television public service announcement produced by CDR Communications, Inc. of Burke, Virginia. The PSA was distributed to the six networks, 1,400 local television stations, and 100 cable networks, reaching a projected total of 20 to 30 million households. The

Dickman's dream. They helped me give $77,000 in scholarship money to seventy-seven outstanding deaf students.

Gradually, thanks to the help of positive people like Donna, my negative image in the deaf community was being dispelled. But not everyone was excited about these new aspects of my work. One deaf organization was so angry about me giving awards to speaking deaf students instead of signing deaf students that they demanded that I quit addressing deaf issues until I surrendered my title. I responded by telling them that I would not quit, because speaking deaf students deserved to be recognized by the Alexander Graham Bell Association for the Deaf, an organization that emphasizes oral education. I further told them that I would be glad to help them give scholarships to deaf students who excelled in sign language skills, but I never heard from them again.

While in Baltimore, I was fortunate enough to meet Alexander Graham Bell's great-grandson, James Watson. I was deeply honored to meet him, and thought that he actually looked a great deal like his great-grandfather. Most people think of Alexander Graham Bell as the inventor of the telephone, but they don't know that his wife and mother were deaf. His invention of the telephone was, in fact, an attempt to help his loved ones' hearing.

From a movie I once watched about Bell's life, I remember a scene where he was walking outside with his wife. He went over to a goat, then lifted the animal's ear and stared at it. "What are you doing?" his wife asked.

"I'm trying to figure out a way to fix your hearing," he told her.

She told him he was being ridiculous because he was more worried about her deafness than she was. She could talk and read lips very well.

As part of their effort to continue Bell's work today, the

Alexander Graham Bell Association for the Deaf sent announcements to their state organizations, urging deaf students to apply for what was officially known as the Alexander Graham Bell Association for the Deaf Heather Whitestone 75 Stars Awards. The awards program was announced in the Bell association magazine, *Volta Voices*, and STARS candidates had to demonstrate a potential for leadership, have a profound hearing loss, and be nominated by one of the AG Bell Association chapter members as well as recommended by a teacher. Nominees eight years old and over were asked to submit an essay describing how my selection as Miss America had affected his or her dreams. More than five hundred young deaf students were nominated for the awards, and all of them received personal letters from me and a special certificate. Every one of those young people was a winner in my eyes.

I was awed at the response, and frankly chagrined when I saw that some of the young nominees had accomplished more than I did. At the first awards ceremony hosted by the Jean Weingarten Peninsula Oral School and the California chapter of the Alexander Graham Bell Association for the Deaf, the cameras flashed while the video cameras churned, but this time I was giving out the prizes, not receiving them. In my hands I held several envelopes, each containing the name of a student who would receive a $1000 savings bond, a medal engraved with a star and the five points of my STARS program, and my congratulatory good wishes. I was so proud of them, and so grateful to have an opportunity to touch their lives.

The seventy-seven young winners were truly remarkable. They ranged in age from six to nineteen and attended a wide range of public and private schools across the United States and Canada. All had oral communication skills and used these skills as their primary mode of communication. Some also knew and used sign language. Some of them were athletes, honor roll students, actors, musicians, singers, leaders in student government, and volunteers who did everything from working in hospitals to building homes for the homeless. And every single one of them aspired to move beyond the deaf world and join the world at large.

Among the deaf students I met and presented with awards in various ceremonies across the country were:

- From Redwood City, California, Alex Zernovoj, sixteen, built homes to help the homeless in Tijuana. He hopes to study business and accounting.
- Renee Goldschmid, fifteen, a National Merit scholar from Redwood City with a 4.0 grade-point average. She hopes to study law and become a U.S. Supreme Court justice. She was a violinist with the El Camino Youth Symphony and a recipient of the Eagle Award for outstanding leadership, academics, community service, and school spirit.
- From Palo Alto, California, Anna Hsuan, sixteen, is fluent in Chinese, English, and French. She traveled to Taiwan and gave a speech—a message of struggle and hope—to the parents of hearing-impaired children.
- Courtney Lynn Payton, a twelve-year-old from San Jose, dreams of becoming a famous singer. She has severe hearing loss, but she sings in her church choir, dances ballet, and is an active gymnast.
- Michael Zullo, sixteen, and from Wallingford, Pennsylvania, is an "all-American boy." His dream is to become a surgeon or cardiologist. He traveled to Australia and New Zealand as the first American hearing-impaired student ambassador in the nationwide "People to People" program. He has won numerous academic honors.
- From Springfield, Pennsylvania, Melissa Pardo, sixteen, was nominated not just for her success as an outstanding English

student, but also because of her keen desire to be helpful to her fellow man.

- Sarah Exley, an eight-year-old from Ambler, Pennsylvania, studied piano, was active in her Brownie troop, and excelled in several subjects at school. "I know everything has not been easy," she told *The Philadelphia Inquirer*. She added that when she was afraid, she enjoyed thinking of Miss America. "It helps me to try my hardest in everything I do."
- Antonio Soto, eight, was a third grader from Philadelphia just three steps away from earning a black belt in karate. (I told him I was glad he wasn't my brother, or I'd have bruises for sure!)

Reaching for the STARS

In an 1859 speech, Carl Schurz said, "Ideals are like stars; you will not succeed in touching them with your hands. But like the seafaring man on the desert of waters, you choose them as your guides, and following them you will reach your destiny."

That quote sums up my feelings about the seventy-five remarkable students who were recognized in those awards ceremonies. They epitomize my STARS program: They are positive people, they have great support teams, they are willing to work hard, they have realistically faced their limitations, and they are committed to following their dreams. And I for one am convinced that they will reach their destinies.

At the Denver 75 STARS awards ceremonies, a troupe of beautiful young deaf dancers performed onstage. The dance was interesting because none of them could hear the music, but they were all dancing around one hearing dancer who guided them through the music. The sight reminded me of old times, when I danced on the stage as a young girl. I was so enthusiastic and proud, I demanded attention from the audience! I used to dance through the grocery store, twirling and whirling for anyone who'd stop and watch. But these dancers were so beautiful and humble.

Someone told me that two of the dancers, nine-year-old Cathleen Arnt and eight-year-old Katie Clawson, had never danced before they watched me win my title. They were quick to notice my hearing aid on television because they wore hearing aids themselves. And now, as they twirled for me in tutus and silver crowns, Cathleen's mother turned and said, "They figured if you could do it, why couldn't they try?"

Another mother from Alabama once shared that her little *hearing* girl dressed up as Miss America for Halloween. She wore a white dress, a sash, a crown, and carried a scepter, but when it came time to go out with her mother, the little girl stopped at the door. "I'm not ready," she said. "I'm not Miss America."

"But, honey," the bewildered mother said. "You've got everything you need—the dress, the crown, the scepter. What else do you want?"

"A hearing aid!" the little girl answered.

Though I enjoyed meeting all children, it was a great delight and pleasure to encourage students with disabilities. At the 75 STARS awards ceremony held at the Tucker Maxon Oral School in Portland, Oregon, I met Vaughn Brown, a seven-year-old boy who is both blind and deaf. For weeks his mother had been preparing him for my visit to his school, telling him that Miss America wore a crown on her head.

"A clown?" he kept asking, not understanding the concept of a crown.

As much as she tried to explain it, Vaughn couldn't grasp the concept.

I was battling exhaustion, as always, when I entered the

Tucker Maxon school, and, aware of the criticism even this great program had produced, I was beginning to wonder if I was doing much good at all as Miss America. But I was carrying my crown as always, ready to display it to the students. I'd learned that carrying instead of wearing it made a better impression. I used it as a visual aid during my STARS presentation, and I wanted people to see my heart and not just have a memory of me standing in front of them with a crown on my head.

As I began to greet the children and shake their hands, Donna Dickman pulled me aside and told me that Vaughn was blind as well as deaf.

"He's been wondering all week why Miss America would wear a clown on her head," she told me.

I walked over to stand in front of Vaughn and then knelt in front of him. Holding the crown, I gently placed it in Vaughn's hands and let him feel it. "A crown," I said, speaking the word loud enough for him to hear through his hearing aid.

What happened next must surely have been like that day when Anne Sullivan spelled w-a-t-e-r into Helen Keller's palm and she suddenly grasped the concept of words. Vaughn's hands scrambled over the framework and the rhinestones, then his little face lit up with joy.

5 Letters to Miss America

Henry David Thoreau once wrote: "I have received no more than one or two letters in my life that were worth the postage."

I'm happy to report that my experience was (happily) quite a bit better than Thoreau's in regard to letters. One of the nicest things about becoming Miss America was receiving letters—hundreds and hundreds of them. There were so many, in fact, that I had to enlist my family and friends to help me answer them all. Because I was constantly on the move, there was no way I could sit down and personally answer the thousands of letters I received, but I did enjoy them very much and responded to as many as I could.

Letters came from every state in the Union, and from the Philippines, South Korea, Japan, Canada, India, New Zealand, Austria, Germany, and England. Some letters arrived on expensive stationery, others were the crayoned scrawlings of preschoolers. But I loved all of them—well, almost all. I suppose every celebrity receives his or her share of strange letters, and I had a few. But most of them were from wonderful, warm people who wrote to share their hearts with me.

Among the letters was a note scrawled with the message, "Happy New Year from Japan!" The envelope had been addressed to "Miss Hezar Whitestone, United States of America, Miss America Contest 1994, New Jersey." I salute our postal service for making sure that letter found its way to me!

A letter from a fifteen-year-old boy in India gave me pause. Calling me "sister," he wrote for my autograph and said:

> *If you are not in a position to send your autograph, I have no option but to commit suicide. No, sister, I am not blackmailing you. Please try to understand how much I respect you. The moment I receive your autograph will be the best moment in my life and I will be the happiest man on this planet. I will treat your autograph as a big great gift from a big great lady to an ordinary guy. I will be carrying a treasure in the form of your autograph that will keep me happy for the rest of my life. Sister, I assure you that your autograph will be treated as ancestral treasure, a most proud treasured possession of our family and that I will hand it over to my children in my deathbed and I will command them to do the same. . . .*

And I had thought autographs were not really a big deal!

Though some of the letters were a bit unusual, others were encouraging. Toyomi Sato, a sixteen-year-old student at Numazu Higashi High School in Japan, sent me a personal note as well as a copy of the speech she had given in an English speech contest. Toyomi won fourth prize, and sent me a copy of her speech. *Her* success inspired *me*!

Here's an excerpt from her English speech:

> . . . I am one of the girls who wants to be a beauty. I have tried and failed again and again. I used up all the money I had to buy newly advertised creams. I ate only apples for five days, I

rubbed my face with cream, I exercised with a video produced by a supermodel, I stopped eating dinner . . . I tried every possible means, but in vain.

One day, I hated my looks and lost all confidence in myself. "Why am I too ugly and fat? I wish I were a supermodel! They are so beautiful and slim." I sighed deeply. To take my mind off my problems, I turned on the TV. That moment a very beautiful woman smiling softly like an angel caught my eye. "Wow, what a beautiful woman she is! Is she a supermodel or a new actress?" . . . Then the announcer said, "The Miss America of 1995, a representative of Alabama, is Heather Whitestone. She is the first Miss America to be a profoundly deaf person. . . ."

I could not believe my ears! Because I thought a handicap would have made her oppressed. However, she smiled beautifully, full of confidence. Her smile made me feel like she had no handicap. . . . So I sent a letter to Miss America, Heather Whitestone, asking the secret of her beauty. But I was anxious if she would answer the letter written by a strange Japanese girl like me who suddenly asked her the secret of being beautiful.

Two months later, I got a reply from Miss America. She said this in her letter, "To me, when you have a beautiful heart and a nice smile, you become beautiful. Believe in yourself first. Don't lose your way, be natural." She told me that a beautiful heart is more important than a beautiful appearance.

Now I understand why she is beautiful. I think her beauty comes across as natural simply because her personality comes across as sincere. I learned what a true beauty is from her. I think the desire to be beautiful can make a person look either desperate or natural depending on the heart of the person in the question.

Of course, caring about your appearance is important. But, before you wear tons of makeup or work hard on a crazy diet, peer into your heart. Is it beautiful? Is it shining? If it is, you are a true beauty. Your looks reflect your heart. If your heart is beautiful, you will be beautiful.

Susan Bailey of Los Alamos, New Mexico, wrote to say that she usually didn't watch pageants because they seemed "superficial and political." But her thirteen-year-old daughter watched me dance and called her mother to the television set. "We watched together," wrote Mrs. Bailey:

> *with goose bumps at your beautiful interpretation and your courageous stand for Christ in front of our whole nation, where sadly that is no longer popular. It still brings a tear to my eye. We continued to watch and learned that you are hearing impaired. I had to get my fifteen-year-old son involved at this point, because he is also hearing impaired. He can hear normally out of one ear, but thinks it a terrible handicap to not be able to hear out of the other one. He tries very hard to be just like everybody else his age, so won't wear a hearing aid, and really does get down on himself . . .*

Mrs. Bailey added that one of her favorite Bible verses was Mark 10:27, "All things are possible with God." That's one of my favorites too!

I was greatly encouraged to hear from Vanessa Mori of Pittsburgh, Pennsylvania. She has two children: a son, Ryan, and a daughter, Erin. Both had been involved in an oral deaf education program. Mrs. Mori wrote:

> *I am personally so delighted for your crown because everyone I encounter assumes that my children know or should know sign language. Many people feel I am demanding "my world" on my children and tell me, "they are deaf, why would you insist that they fit into your world?" Well, your crown is opening eyes and helping people realize that there are options for deaf people. There is not one way you must go because you are deaf. I'm so glad you talk about both*

methods of communication and freely use both. You are an inspira-
tion to all people to be all they can be no matter what. . . .

From Redding, California, Kathy Kushell's letter made me
glad that I was helping with the early detection program. "Our
family was blessed one year ago with a beautiful baby," she
wrote, "Danielle, who we discovered three and a half months
after her birth, is hearing impaired. . . . We are fortunate she
was born in the nineties and not fifty years ago, when she would
have been left in her isolated world!"

Mrs. Karen Kaser and her daughter, Kate, of Castle Rock,
Colorado, reminded me of myself as a child—always slaving
over homework! Kate is a perfect example of a STAR!

"The day you became Miss America," Mrs. Kaser wrote:

my daughter was sitting doing her fall break school homework. She
was comparing her regular education homework (nine pages) to her
hearing impaired class work (80 pages) and complaining—wishing
her ears were normal.

Then, like any eight-year-old girl, Kate wanted to watch the
Miss America Pageant. Kate just knew you would win—even though
I kept saying you may not. I didn't want her too disappointed.

Kate thought you had such a "pretty voice" and that she could
understand you better because she is hard of hearing also. Then,
when you did your ballet for the talent competition, again our Miss
Kate was so thrilled because she takes dance lessons.

And when you won—Kate and I had tears in our eyes and I
told her, "See, you can be anything." She really believed it and
wanted to know if she could be president. I said yes! From day one
we have always taught Kate the glass was half full, not half empty.
Thank God for her and us, because Kate was misdiagnosed until she
was four years old. She had virtually no speech. Kate has a moderate
to severe hearing loss and we use total communication. We are col-
lege-educated, caring parents, but we were unfortunately surrounded

for the first four years with doctors and childhood therapists who said
Kate was slow, lazy, retarded, or that I didn't make her talk.

The next four years has been a full court press, intensive speech
therapy, sign language, and constant work. Last month Kate finally
learned to say "school" instead of "cool." I am one proud mother!

Not only did I hear from the parents of deaf children, but deaf people themselves wrote me scores of letters. Martha Askins, of Charlotte, North Carolina, wrote: "I didn't for a minute believe they would select a deaf girl [to win the Miss America pageant], and I thought you were pretty 'gutsy' to even enter the contest. I have Menière's disease and severe bilateral hearing loss. I have felt 'diminished' because of my hearing deficit and I am careful to wear my hair so that it covers my hearing aid. . . . I couldn't believe you wore your hair in an upswept style, but I do admire your confidence and guts!"

Sheiba Tafazzoli, of Chatsworth, California, wrote: "I was born hearing. When I was almost four I got a disease. I could have died! I can talk just like a hearing person. One time my hair was covering my ears and I asked someone, 'You think I am hearing or deaf?' And she said, 'Hearing' because I talk good. . . . I hope you enjoyed my letter!"

The brightest letters always came from children. Several elementary schools in Alabama "adopted" me as a class project, and I received lots of beautiful, glittery portraits of me in colorful gowns and crowns. Children's letters are always a delight, as you can see from this small sampling:

Dear Heather Whitestone:
Every Friday in our English class a guest speaker reads part of a
book to us. It only takes about fifteen minutes. When you're at the
school it will be period four which starts at 10:35. You will have to
bring your own book. We would love for you to come.
                              Nicole Icholnyit, Merrick, New York

Hi, Heather Whitestone:
> I am deaf just like you, did you know that? All about me:
> Hair: little, blonde
> Eyes: chocolate
> Skin: tan
> Age: eleven
> Birthday: March 21, 1983
> Likes: cats, dogs, horses
> Don't likes: bugs, mices, chickens
> Tall: little tall
> Small: no
> Medium: yes
> Weight: seventy-five pounds
> Can you tell me about you? Who are your hearing friends?
When did you go to the contest? What do you do on the weekends?
>   Your best friend, Emily, Oakridge Elementary,
>   Salt Lake City, Utah

Dear Miss Whitestone:
> Hi. I saw you on The 700 Club and I thought it was awesome
to see how much you love God. . . . See, I thought Christians
couldn't be famous because famous people usually have high egos of
themselves. My mom says that you can't love yourself and God. But
watching you I realized that if you ask God and keep praying, God
can let you win Miss America or something. Miss Whitestone, I
have never had anything big to overcome. I never realized how hard
it was to say a sound without hearing it. You are my role model. I
want to be a STAR and have five points just like you teach.
>   Sarah Band, Hudson, New Hampshire

Dear Heather Whitestone:
> My name is Angela. I am deaf like you. In school we are learn-
ing how to keep score with a spare and strikes in bowling. I wrote a
mystery called "Under the Rug." Here is what I look like: my hair

is blonde, eyes are green, I wear pink glasses. I became deaf from coming out early and I was very sick. I almost died. I was very lucky I didn't die. I am glad.

    Angela Neilson, Oakridge Elementary, Salt Lake City, Utah

Dear Miss America:

    I'm eleven years old and in the sixth grade at City Park School. In my class we are writing people who are famous or people we admire. I admire you. . . . If you have time, I would like you to write back. I know you're busy, but I do get extra credit if you do.

    Brittany Gordon, Dalton, Georgia

One elementary school class sent me a package of letters in which they explained that from my example they had learned the value of practicing to fulfill their dreams. They told me that they wanted to become everything from baseball players to ballerinas, and they promised to work hard and practice a lot. The following letter was from that class:

Dear Miss Whitestone:

    Congratulations! I like to play soccer. When I was playing soccer I made twenty points. I was trying to get the ball, but somebody kicked me in my face. But my head made a score. My mom and everybody that was on my team started to slap me five. They asked me how did you do it? I said that I was practicing.

    Love, Kris

Dear Heather:

    I go to East Elementary School. You came here once. You are a nice dancer. Do you like hockey? I do. My favorite player is Wayne Gretzky, he plays for the Los Angeles Kings. For coming to our school I want to give you my Wayne Gretzky card. Please keep it safe.

    Love, Justin Heston, Cullman, Alabama

(He did send me his prized card, and, Justin, I'm keeping it safe for you!)

Dear Miss Whitestone:

My name is Megan St. Denis. I'm fourteen years of age and a freshman at Robinson High School. I am profoundly deaf and wear hearing aids in both ears. I have put up with a lot of teasing because of my hearing aids. But I have always found a way to put that behind me. Because I am different I feel that I have to prove myself to the world that even though I am handicapped I can do everything everyone can. I enjoy talking on the phone and trying to make everyone else's lives easier. Sometimes I achieve that and sometimes I don't.

My dream is to go to college and major in business, then go to law school. . . . I think it is great that you overcame your deafness and achieved your dream. It just shows that even though you are different you can achieve anything you want out of life. You can get it if you try hard enough for it. The one thing in life I have learned about being impaired is that sometimes there are people out there who want to hurt you, but you have to look past those people and look toward your true friends. They are the ones who stick by you no matter what the rest of the world thinks about you. Gotta flex!

Love always, Megan St. Denis, a.k.a. "Little Blondie"

Dear Miss America:

I am glad you won. I know how you feel. Did you know that I take clogging? I appreciate what you have done for us. Did you know what? I was born with my skull showing. I had to have a skin graph. I had to wear a bandage for three years. It was hard for me. When I was a baby I had to see the doctor for my head every week. Now I have to every year. Soon I will have to get surgery to get hair on top of my head. I want to let you know how I feel about you. I am sorry you are deaf. It is really hard, isn't it?

Love, Lauren Allon

Dear Heather:

Me and my mom watched you win Miss America. You should have seen my mom when you won! She was so excited when you won she was jumping on the sofa cheering for you!

Yours truly, Natasha Zenanko, Jacksonville, Alabama

Dear Heather Whitestone:

Congratulations for breaking their hearts. I am Austin Minter of Anniston, Alabama. In school on my report card I make all A's. I've never made a B in my life. As you can see, I am pretty smart. I hope you will remember me.

Sincerely, Austin Minter, Jacksonville, Alabama

Dear Mrs. Umerka:

I'm so glad that you are Mrs. Umerka I could jump in mashed butter and swim.

Your friend, Leslie

I was even honored with poetry!

For Heather, Miss America:

People doubted you from the start,
Memorizing music at first with a dart,
But then you listened to your heart.

You showed America what you can do,
Ballet dancing was nothing new,
But ballet the way you do,
Was new.

Your good personality and willingness to do
Things that no one thought you could do,
Your ballet dancing is more than a trifle,
Equals "Miss Alabama, you've won a new title!"

6 Learning to Live Under Pressure

*A*s spring lengthened into summer days, I went home to crown a new Miss Alabama and spend a little time with my family. I knew I wouldn't be able to relax the way I wanted to, but I had finished most of my term. I told myself I'd be able to take a true vacation after I gave up my crown and title in September.

Immediately after the Miss Alabama Pageant, my family and I wanted to go out for dinner together. We chose a nice Birmingham restaurant where the manager recognized me. I don't hear the buzzing that goes on in a public place, but somehow everyone in the restaurant learned that Miss America and her family were eating dinner there.

Before we even had a chance to order, people began coming up and asking for autographs. I smiled and signed whatever they thrust at me, but after a while I got frustrated. The nice family dinner I'd looked forward to was rapidly turning into just another autograph session. I had so little time to be with my family, and I couldn't concentrate on them with scores of people around.

My traveling companion talked to the manager, and he tried to stop the flood of people. Bonnie, my companion that month, had a stack of small autographed photos in her purse, and in an effort to give me a little private time with my family, she gave these to the people standing in line.

Apparently that wasn't good enough. One mother with two little children by her side stormed forward to confront the manager. "This isn't right," she told him, lifting her chin. "You can't stop us from meeting her. We aren't leaving until my kids have met Miss America. And we want our picture taken with her."

The manager, apologetic now, came to our table and said he had an angry mother on his hands. What could I do? I let her and her children come over and smiled while someone snapped a picture. But she was still angry when she left. And the next day an article in the local newspaper reported the episode and made me sound rude and snobby.

I just wanted to eat dinner with my family in peace!

Fame can be a two-edged sword. While it can cut through a lot of red tape, it can also be turned on you. People seemed to think that Miss America belongs to them, and I can understand that feeling. I felt that way myself when I was a little girl. A man called out "I love you, will you marry me?" to Debbye Turner, Miss America 1990, as she walked down the runway just after being crowned in Atlantic City. The man apparently assumed her wave to the crowd meant yes. He packed up his things, moved to California, and then had the gall to sue her for breach of promise when she didn't go to California and marry him!

America has high expectations for its Atlantic City sweetheart. Terry Meeuwsen had told me that the hardest part about her year was living up to the public's image. Some people had such unrealistic expectations. They expected me to step off every airplane looking like I'd just come from the pageant runway, with a dozen unwiltable roses in my arms, my makeup perfectly in place, my hair shiny and topped by a glittering crown. Sometimes I thought they imagined that I went to Atlantic City on a whim and won the competition because a fairy godmother waved her magic wand over my head. They didn't realize it took me three years of hard work to win the crown.

I was always around people who expected me to look and act and talk and perform up to their standards—which were pretty high.

One time in North Dakota—an unusual place for a Miss America to visit—I needed to go to the rest room after the plane landed. Miss America's arrival in New York City is no big deal, but things are different in the great state of North Dakota! My traveling companion and I met our hostess, then I excused myself and went into the rest room.

After a moment I heard a high-pitched squeal from outside the stall. I didn't know what was going on, but suddenly a big green eyeball was peering at me through the crack in the door frame.

I froze. Nothing in my pageant experience had taught me how to gracefully handle a female peeping Tom. The eyeball disappeared, and I sighed in relief. A moment later, when I was at the sink washing my hands, a strong woman grabbed me in a bear hug, then ran into the stall I'd just vacated and closed the door. I don't want to *begin* guessing why.

Mickey was stunned. I asked her what was going on, and she said a woman had been screaming, "Where's Miss America?" and then looked for me through the crack. I couldn't believe what had just happened, and neither could Mickey.

Another time when I was in Alabama during the governor's inauguration, I entered a crowded rest room. I was in a relaxed, festive mood until suddenly, like football players, a group of women rushed toward me, wanting my autograph. I signed a few, then hurried into a stall and was horrified when a woman slipped a piece of paper to me under the door. There was no escape!

I regret this now, but my temper flared. I walked out of the bathroom to the sink, trying to hurry and get out of there, but women kept pushing paper toward me—and one woman nearly pushed me into the sink. "Stop it!" I yelled, turning.

That did it. Like a group of frightened birds, they retreated, their bright eyes blinking in surprise.

It was wrong of me to lose my temper; I made a mistake. Even though they shouldn't have been pushing me, I'm sure they'll always remember me losing my cool in the bathroom. If I had that day to live all over again, I'd try to bite my tongue . . . (or maybe use the men's room with my companion standing guard outside the door!).

I was hurrying toward a car to take me to a television studio in Ohio, when a man held up two index cards and asked for an autograph. Bonnie took my arm and led me toward the car, telling him that we were late and didn't have time to stop. I climbed into the car, then glanced back at the man. I read his lips—he was cursing at us.

"Bonnie," I said, disturbed, "why is he cursing at us?"

"That's his problem, not yours, Heather," she said, closing the car door. "Don't worry about him."

But I did worry. Though I was trying to be the best Miss America I could be, I kept making people angry.

I never really saw the big deal behind autographs; I didn't like asking for them from the celebrities I met. But if I didn't stop and do signings when people asked, I'd read about it in the paper the next day—someone would write in and complain about the snobby Miss America representing our country. The trouble with autographs is that once you agree to do one, a hundred other people are emboldened to come up and ask for your signature. A thirty-second task becomes a thirty-minute ordeal, and once you begin, there's no graceful way to cut waiting people off and call a halt. And some people threw a fit if I didn't spell their name correctly, or didn't sign six copies of something for all their relatives.

Though some dealings with people were difficult, there were other people who went far beyond the call of duty to make my appearances special and successful. My first weekend to visit Alabama after winning the crown was more enjoyable than I could have imagined. So many wonderful people drove long distances to show their support.

I didn't learn until much later how much some of my friends had suffered to make that homecoming weekend special. My good friend, Jim Davis, told me about his experience. His job was to take care of the parade, and he said it was a nightmare! Among his many problems was a woman who wanted to send her little "bees" (girls in costume) to "buzz" around my float. Well, of course you can't have little children running in front of moving vehicles. It just isn't safe. When Jim explained, the woman was so angry, she told him she would call the government to complain. Jim promptly gave her a government phone number . . . for the IRS!

No one ever promised that following a dream would be easy . . . just worth it. I think Mickey, Bonnie, and I all had trying moments during my year as Miss America. At different points I cried out my frustrations to my two traveling companions. Sometimes the public frustrated me, at other times I'd get upset over being misquoted or misunderstood. Mickey would say, "Heather, let it go! You can't worry and obsess over every little thing. Enjoy your year, and don't worry so much about what people think. One year as Miss America is very short."

Bonnie and Mickey

I don't know what I would have done without my two traveling companions. They are mature women whose children are grown, and their job is to act partly as bodyguard, partly as chaperon. In my case they also became my interpreters . . . and my friends. Whenever I answered questions before a large crowd, there were always some people who were so far away, I couldn't read their lips. On those occasions I'd just look at Mickey or Bonnie, and they would repeat the question for me. When I was doing autographs, Mickey or Bonnie stood beside me and always asked the next person in line for his or her name. They would write it down for me so I could get the spelling right. Little things like that were very helpful.

Some people have asked if having a constant companion around was sometimes annoying, but I can honestly say there was never a time I didn't want one of my companions with me. I relied on their valuable experience; Bonnie had been a Miss America traveling companion for six years, Mickey had traveled for three. They alternated months of traveling with me, and though I loved them, I always got a little peeved the night before they were to leave for their month at home. I'd try to make them feel guilty by saying things like "How dare you leave me and go home! I'm so jealous! For a month you won't have to haul around a trunk, you can eat anything you want to, and you'll have free time while I'm stuck in a hotel. . . ." Did they ever feel guilty? Not a bit!

The Miss America traveling companion helps with crowd

control, hotel reservations, itineraries, and whatever else comes up. Bonnie and Mickey have very different personalities. Sometimes I thought they behaved a little like guard dogs, at least in public. They kept people in an orderly line while they waited for autographs and weren't afraid to say no when it needed to be said. They'd say, "It's your job to be sweet, and my job to be mean," but in private they were as sweet as angels. They never wanted to be in my spotlight, not even when I wanted them to be in it with me. At all the fancy dinners to which I was invited, I'd always ask for my traveling companion to sit with me at the head table if possible, but Bonnie and Mickey hated that kind of attention—and I can understand why. Who wants to sit on an elevated platform while people watch you eat?

Mickey is a relatively serious person, she never gave me advice unless I asked for it. She treated me with respect, and though she didn't always agree with me, she kept quiet about her difference of opinion unless I asked for her views.

Bonnie's personality always made me laugh. She had a great sense of humor, and often told me that she was getting younger as her children got older. Whenever I had a problem, she'd say, "Heather, get a life. Think positive."

Sometimes when we'd be riding in a limo with darkened windows, Bonnie would have fun by rolling down the window slightly and then extending her hand in a genteel little wave. People would point and scream, "Look! Miss America's waving to us!" Little did they know that I was giggling on the other side of the car.

"Bonnie," I asked once after wiping tears of laughter from my eyes. "Do you do this all the time?"

"When I feel like it," she said, grinning as she put the window up.

In April I was invited to make a presentation at the Acad-

emy of Country Music awards. When Mickey and I arrived at
our hotel, we found that our rooms were not ready. Mickey
checked her watch—time was short. We still had to go to a
rehearsal, and we didn't think we'd have time to come back to
the hotel. So Mickey took one of my evening gowns out of the
suitcase and slipped it into her purse. That night I wore that
gown for a television audience of millions, and it didn't have a
single wrinkle! Mickey had come through again. When faced
with sticky situations, my companions knew how to improvise!

On July fourth, Mickey and I were staying at a hotel in
Washington, D.C. As we settled down and got ready for bed, I
smelled something strange in my bedroom—sort of a chemical
smell. I called out to see if Mickey smelled it too.

Mickey went straight to the phone. I did not know what
she said, but within five minutes I heard the sirens from a fire
truck outside. I didn't panic because I often heard sirens in
Washington, but just a few minutes later someone knocked on
the door of our suite. When Mickey opened it, a fireman stood
outside, complete with fire hose and face mask. "Oh, my goodness!" I screamed. "What's going on?"

After they checked our room and my heart returned to its
normal steady beat, I asked Mickey why in the world she called
the fire department. "I didn't, Heather," she said. "I only called
the front desk. But it's better to be safe than sorry."

I don't know what I'd have done without Bonnie and
Mickey. I confided in them and unburdened my heart to them.
When I wanted to scream because the job was stressful, they
allowed me to scream in the hotel. We always ate our meals
together, so we talked a lot. I knew I could trust them with my
secrets. Of course, they did talk freely about my public positions, but they always kept quiet about my personal problems
and my greatest joys.

An Uncomfortable Hero

I had found some of my greatest joys in the sacks of mail I received from around the world. I received thousands of letters, and I adored hearing from children and deaf students who said my example challenged them to strive for their dreams.

I didn't feel worthy of such praise. I had only followed my dream and God had set me on this journey, so it seemed strange that so many people would think of me as a hero. The idea of anyone idolizing me made me uncomfortable, and I tended to dismiss the flowery comments even as I fretted over negative criticism. I've heard it said that we can be given nine compliments and one rebuke, and it's always the rebuke we'll remember. That is certainly how I felt.

I was very honored to be invited to the Birmingham Southern College Gala 12, a function designed to "honor outstanding women in the arts and media." The honorees included bestselling novelist Barbara Taylor Bradford, Emmy-award–winning actress Lynda Carter, president of the Peter F. Drucker Foundation Frances Hesselbein, U.S. Senator Kay Bailey Hutchinson, NBC News correspondent Gwen Ifill, retired bishop Leontine Kelly, artist Ida Kohlmeyer, author and lecturer Bette Bao Lord, Tony-award–winning actress Phyllis Newman, former surgeon general Antonia Novello, M.D., social scientist Elisabeth Kübler-Ross, White House press correspondent Helen Thomas, and . . . me.

I felt like a fish out of water among those remarkable women. They were all more polished and mature than I was. I thought I must have seemed very young to them because they were so accomplished. They did greet me warmly, and we talked a bit.

I appreciated the great honor Birmingham Southern College bestowed on me by including me with those incredible, intelligent, and hardworking women, but in my heart I didn't feel that I'd done anything to deserve being included among them. Yes, I have worked hard to follow my dream, but every dream requires a price of the one who follows it.

After the Gala 12, I honestly felt guilty. In my hands I held a beautiful crystal trophy, but I felt like I'd done nothing to deserve it. Every woman there had given a speech—none of which I could hear—and I'd spent the entire evening smiling and pretending to listen to the program.

One thing in particular struck me that night. Those women, all of whom were great achievers, had fun together. They knew how to work hard, but they also knew how to have a good time. They laughed and joked with one another, and seemed to really enjoy their jobs.

More and more I was finding it difficult to enjoy my job as Miss America. Those women had been in the public eye for years. I'd been a public figure for only nine months, but already I was looking longingly back at those simple days when no one knew me. I couldn't figure out why God had allowed my dream to bring me such despair. I knew there must be a reason, but I couldn't see it. I clung to the belief that he would use my experiences to mold me for something that would happen in the future, because I couldn't see that he was using me at all in the present.

After nights like that one at Birmingham Southern College, I turned to introspection, and my thoughts weren't always healthy. I felt so rushed in our hectic schedule that I neglected my habit of daily prayer and Bible study. By spring I was more likely to spend my quiet moments feeling sorry for myself than I was seeking God's help. I had honestly begun to wonder why in the world I ever became Miss America.

How was I changing lives by signing autographs? How was

I influencing people by sitting at a head table and giving a short speech? I had repeated my STARS motivational speech so many times that it now felt like gibberish.

Those feelings overcame me again at the thirty-fourth annual American Academy of Achievement awards banquet. The dinner was a black-tie affair held at the Williamsburg Lodge, and I found myself sitting at a rose-strewn head table with such honorees as Robin Williams, Bob Woodward, Mike Wallace, Martha Stewart, Rosa Parks, Arnold Palmer, Lady Bird Johnson, Peggy Noonan, the Honorable Ruth Bader Ginsburg, Patricia Cornwell, President George Bush, and other leaders in business and industry.

What in the world could I have done to land an invitation to sit with these people?

The banquet was given for outstanding high school seniors, and our assignment was to share a bit of advice about success and how to find it. My advice was straightforward and simple: "When you enter college, remember that the more freedom you have, the more responsibility you will have."

I sat down, feeling a little silly, and found myself wondering why God had brought me to that place.

In the weeks that followed, I took my eyes off my goal—to be the best Miss America I could be—and began to think about myself. A serious mistake.

It wasn't the first time I'd made that blunder. At Christmas my loving cousin Trey gave me one of those hand-held video games. He knew I would love it, and I thought it'd be a fun way to pass the time while I flew from place to place. But I soon discovered that I concentrated so hard on the game that I was completely unaware of what was going on around me. (Being deaf had always blocked a great deal of awareness. The video game took it all!)

I took that game seriously and my competitive personality

drove me to play it with deep concentration. Once, while I was playing in the airport, a student approached. Bonnie tapped me on the shoulder, and my first reaction was to rudely turn and snap "What?"

A mistake. I carried that game with me for about a month and a half, then the voice of God spoke to my heart: "You've got to stop this, you've got to stop playing this game in public. You're not being the best Miss America you can be."

So I put it away, out of sight in the suitcase, and pulled it out only when I was alone. I remembered how Bob Dole had made me feel special by giving me his undivided attention, and remembered that I'd promised myself to be respectful to other people in that same way. It wasn't easy to give up my wants and make other people happy, but that video game taught me that you have to make sacrifices to show respect.

But the pace of Miss America's life left me feeling like I was in a tornado. I didn't have a lot of time to stop and consider all the lessons I was learning, or even think deeply about the incredible people I'd met. Often I had no idea where I was or where I was going.

Once I was in Minnesota, speaking to a group of elementary-school students. I always tried to be at my sharpest when I was with students because they look for heroes and I wanted to motivate them to dream, work hard, and stay in school.

The principal introduced me, and I began to take questions from the students. One girl asked, "How do you become Miss America?" so I began to explain the pageant system.

"First you enter a local pageant," I said. "For instance, you might win Miss Grand Rapids, then you'll compete for Miss Michigan. And if you win that—"

I paused in mid-sentence. Some of the children were giggling, others had confused looks on their faces. I had a feeling I knew what was wrong.

"Where am I?" I asked, turning to Mickey.

"Heather," she said, trying to smother her own smile. "You're in Minnesota."

I turned back to the children and shrugged. "You see?" I said. "I'm so mixed up, I don't even know where I am."

Another time I was so brain dead that I wore a sleeveless sundress in the middle of winter when our schedule said we were going to Portland, Oregon. Don't blame my geography teacher, but I was so tired, I had this crazy mental picture of Portland being in the south, somewhere next to New Orleans.

Mickey looked at me in that summer dress and said, "Are you going to wear that?"

"Yes," I answered, wondering why she would ask.

She just shrugged. "Okay."

Then we got in the airplane. Two hours later I looked out the window and saw the desert beneath us. "What's going on?" I asked her.

"We are going to Portland," she said, grinning mischievously. "Oregon. That's the western desert out there."

I pulled out a map and saw that Portland was out on the West Coast. And up north.

Sigh.

Role Models

I don't know how other public figures manage so well. One woman whom I adopted as a role model during my Miss America year was Elizabeth Dole. I read an article about her in an airline magazine and was immediately impressed. She was president of the American Red Cross, and in the article she talked about her mission to Africa, where she had met many children who lost their parents in warfare. Their situations broke Elizabeth's heart, and just reading about them broke mine too.

I was particularly interested in Mrs. Dole because she had worked in several political offices under President Reagan before she accepted her job as president of the Red Cross. *Here is a woman who is truly helping to make this a better world*, I told myself. *How can I be more like her?*

I'd been resisting the idea of influencing people through politics because I don't like political games. But Elizabeth Dole, a woman with a law degree, certainly had to deal with political game-playing, and yet she still remained committed to helping others. I found myself hoping that I'd get a chance to meet her, and when I confessed that desire to Mary McGinnis, the director of corporate community relations for the Miss America Organization, she called Mrs. Dole's office and arranged a meeting.

I was amazed and grateful that someone as busy as Elizabeth Dole would make time in her tight schedule for me. When I first met her, I felt the same warmth about her that I had noticed when I met her husband, Bob Dole. Knowing that she had a hectic schedule, I would have been grateful if she had only five minutes to spare for me. I imagined that we'd talk briefly and have a picture taken together, but when I got to her lovely office, she had tea and cookies waiting on the table. We sat on the couch and talked for almost an hour.

What struck me the most about Elizabeth Dole was her great love for the work of the American Red Cross. She has earned a law degree and is a very successful politician. The American Red Cross has nothing to do with her political work or the practice of law. She told me that she believes money and fame do not bring people joy. Only those who love others find joy in their jobs.

She also thanked me for standing up for Jesus. "I, too, am a Christian," she said.

As I was saying my farewells, I thanked her for her time. Mrs. Dole smiled. A year later I read her book, *Unlimited Partners*, and learned that she had once approached a busy woman, who took time for her. She promised herself that she'd do the same for other women who sought her help.

God was bringing all sorts of powerful and influential women into my life. If I had to choose two women who were my "women of the year," I'd have to select Elizabeth Dole and Marva Collins, a nationally known teacher from inner-city Chicago. Ms. Collins operates a private school and is very strict with her students. She believes her children are no different from others. She tells them, "You have the same equipment that Martin Luther King had, that the President and other successful people have. You have the same heart and mind, and you can dream a dream just as they did."

Ms. Collins does not allow her students to lapse into black English; she tells them to speak proper English in her classroom. Her principles remind me of my own convictions about deaf education. All students, whether they are black, deaf, or whatever, deserve the best education available. And just as Ms. Collins's students need to speak standard English, deaf students shouldn't concentrate only on the language of the deaf, but should be taught proper English in either sign language or oral speaking so they can communicate in the world beyond the deaf community. Marva Collins's example gave me the strength to continue to stand for my convictions.

Once I had an occasion to meet with a group of doctors who were skilled in cochlear implant surgery. Over and over again I was asked for my views about cochlear implants and if I would agree to have one. At first I politely thanked the doctors for their concern, but said I preferred to wear my hearing aid because with it I could hear music and talk on the phone.

For those of you who aren't familiar with the term, a co-

chlear implant is an electronic device that is surgically im-
planted into the bony structure of a deaf person's inner ear. A
transmitter placed outside the scalp sends signals to a receiver
under the scalp, which then transmits a signal to the auditory
nerve. The implant does not transmit speech clearly, but it
does allow individuals to be aware of sounds that they could
not otherwise hear.

A cochlear implant would not benefit me, but the doctors
continued to question me. I tried to answer them nicely, but
finally my frustration boiled over. "Look—you've got to stop
questioning me about this," I told them. "I can hear with my
hearing aid, so I don't need an implant."

That night, at the 75 STARS awards ceremony in Atlanta,
I met a group of deaf people with cochlear implants. They
asked the same question—would I consider having one?—and
I wondered for a moment if I'd lose my temper with them too.
But, amazingly, God put tactful words on my tongue. "I have
not considered the surgery myself," I told them, "but believe it
has value to build self-esteem and help people become successful in the same way communications options such as sign language, lip reading, and hearing aids do."

God gave me grace on that and many other occasions. People thought I had a wonderful life when I was growing up and
during my Miss America year. I constantly heard, "Oh, you're
so sweet, so wonderful," but trust me, I wanted to answer, "You
may see an angel in public, but I can be a real devil in private."
In private I sometimes rebelled against the expectations, pressure, and obligations I felt from others.

The honors, the accolades, and compliments blended into
such a constant background noise that I wasn't even aware of
them, unless to doubt that I even deserved them. The old insecurities and the loneliness that had plagued me since childhood
began to creep back.

I was lonely. I met new people every day, I was surrounded by people during most of my waking hours, and yet they knew only Miss America, the young woman they'd read about in the newspapers. They didn't know Heather Whitestone. Often they didn't even refer to me by name. They didn't know that the sight of water meeting the sky moves me beyond words, that I am really a very private person, that I dream of dancing as an ice skater and having my very own dog.

This photo of the deaf and blind boy I mention in the book is one of my favorite pictures.

This is when Mickey, Carlene (who worked for Waterford Crystal), and I went bicycling.

The Oscar-winning actress Marlee Matlin (who is also deaf) and I had breakfast together out in California. I was really grateful for her support during some tough times.

This is Kathie Lee Gifford and me at the Super Bowl. There she challenged me to be a Christian in the spotlight.

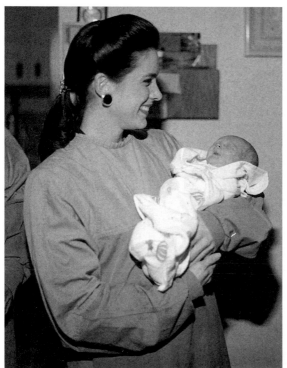

As Miss America I visited many organizations that help people, including a hospital that specializes in the early detection of hearing loss. (No, this is not my baby!)

It had been such a whirlwind year that brought me back to Atlantic City, to dance again, to see Regis and Kathie Lee again, and to crown Miss America 1996, Shawntel Smith.

In the fall of 1996 (after I gave up my title as Miss America), I flew an F-16 at the Wright-Patterson Air Force Base in Ohio.

Even after my responsibilities as Miss America 1995 ended, I was still very busy speaking around the world. I was invited by Citibank to speak in Taiwan.

While I was in Taiwan, I visited one of the foremost private high schools for girls.

John and I were married on June 8, 1996. I'm grateful to God for giving me John as my husband.

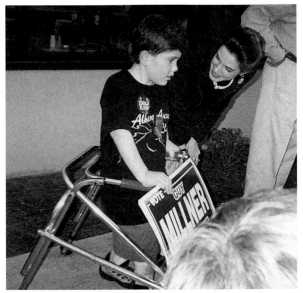

Today I am still active as a speaker and sometimes help support different politicians in their campaigns. Here I'm talking with a sweet boy who was getting an early start in politics in the 1996 election.

One campaign I was particularly involved with was Bob Dole's run for the White House, during which I toured with Senator Dole and addressed the Republican National Convention. Here I am with the senator and John.

John and *I* today.

7 Running on Empty

*I*n April, when *Mademoiselle* magazine asked me to identify my favorite article of clothing, I replied: "My ballet outfit. I have been a ballerina for fifteen years. Since my national speaking tour as Miss America 1995 keeps me traveling twenty thousand miles a month . . . into a different city every other day . . . the moments are precious and few when I can put on my toe shoes and dance. It is during these times that I feel the most free. My movements enable me to feel that there are no limitations to anything I can do."

By the time spring greened into summer, it had been a long time since I'd pulled on my toe shoes . . . and a long time since I had felt the freedom of no limitations. I had worked hard to achieve what I felt was God's dream for me, but much of the joy had gone out of the journey.

In her book *Midstream: My Later Life*, Helen Keller wrote about the frustrations she faced while traveling to her speaking engagements. Once, after leaving cold Salt Lake City, Helen, her mother, and her teacher bundled up in furs to endure the long train ride to Los Angeles. After a train derailment and a sleepless night, they stepped out on the train station platform, where a great gathering of friends, reporters, and photographers greeted them.

"All the ladies present were daintily dressed in summer gowns with flowers on their hats and gay sunshades over their heads," writes Helen. "We were so embarrassed by our appearance that we declined the special automobiles, jumped into a taxi, and told the driver to take us as fast as he could to the Alexandria Hotel. But as he turned the corner, something went wrong with the car, and he had to stop. . . . Instantly reporters sprang upon the running board and demanded an interview, and the photographers caught up with us and pointed their cameras at us! Every effort was made to delay us, but we insisted on going to our hotel. Our friends' feelings were hurt, the newspaper people were indignant, our manager was in a rage. Our rooms were full of exquisite flowers, beautiful fruits, and everything to add to our comfort and pleasure; but we were too exasperated and weary to enjoy them. Indeed, it was several days before we could feel like human beings, and not like wild creatures in a gilded cage."[1]

I know that most people think Miss America's life is wonderfully luxurious. My traveling companion and I did fly first class to our destinations, and we shared lovely hotel suites. But a gilded cage is still a cage, and as the summer leaves began to toast golden brown, I desperately looked forward to freedom.

One of the little boys who wrote me wanted to know what I did on my weekends—the same thing I did on weekdays! In fact, in the thousands of miles I traveled each month, I had very little free time and very few days to call my own. I was

---

[1]Helen Keller, *Midstream: My Later Life* (New York: Doubleday, Doran & Company, Inc., 1929), p. 160.

supposed to have one day off each month, but there were three months when I had no day off at all. And on my rare days off, I couldn't go home. I was confined to the hotel wherever I was, and I usually just collapsed on the bed and did nothing. At the beginning of the year I teased my traveling companions about how lucky they were because they could go home; by June I wasn't teasing anymore. I was dead serious when I asked Bonnie and Mickey, "How can you go off and leave me like this?"

Worst of all, though I was traveling to fabulous places where I met influential and interesting people, everything began to melt together in a blur. One lesson God taught me during my Miss America year is that life is short. "For your life is like the morning fog," writes the apostle James. "It's here a little while, then it's gone." That's what my year was like. I had no time to reflect, to think, barely even to record my thoughts in my journal. After my daily speaking engagements, Bonnie or Mickey and I would go back to our hotel rooms, then I'd fall into bed, trying to get a few hours of sleep before jetting across another time zone or two for another engagement.

I don't want to sound ungrateful, and I never wanted to complain. After all, I had a pretty good idea of what the job would be like when I entered the Miss America Pageant. Just as in Helen Keller's situation, the people who served as my hosts and hostesses were warm, kind, and hospitable. But, increasingly, I became too tired to even notice.

I remember one night in Hawaii—I looked up at the sky and suddenly realized that it was the first time in months that I'd had an opportunity to look up and study the stars. I'd just finished speaking at an Amway convention, and I was given a few days off at the gorgeous Ritz-Carlton Hotel. Bonnie and I slipped out to walk on the beach. Hawaii was so beautiful, and I've always loved the beach because it reminds me of the weekends I spent with my family at Panama City Beach.

So as we walked along the beach, I looked up at the stars and nearly gasped at their beauty. How easily we become distracted and forget! The stars had always symbolized my dreams, and now that I was living one of them, I'd forgotten all about the gift of dreaming . . . and the beauty of wonder.

It's been said that a man gazing on the stars is always at the mercy of puddles in the road. I'd been at the mercy of annoying puddles without even taking the time to stargaze. I was so busy fretting over the routine, the exhaustion, the lack of freedom, I hadn't taken the time to look up and around.

A person's self-esteem plummets when she is tired. And when you've been on an emotional high for a long time, the resulting low can be devastating. My emotional roller coaster was definitely bottoming out, and my return to the Miss Alabama Pageant was uncomfortable. The pageant officials had asked me to dance at the pageant, so I did, but I was out of shape, I had blisters on my feet, and I was in low spirits. I did the best I could, then took my bows. As the enthusiastic applause washed over me on that empty stage, memories of a long-ago afternoon came crowding back. . . .

The year before I was crowned Miss America I spent an afternoon at the Green Valley Elementary School in Hoover, Alabama, where I polished the STARS program by working with the children. My friend Vicki Davis, who is the principal there, had helped me tremendously. She serves a vast variety of students with all her heart and love and wisdom. On the particular day she had invited me to speak, a bell suddenly interrupted my STARS presentation.

"Is it a fire drill?" I asked, looking up.

"No." Vicki smiled and told the children to line up. Intrigued, I followed them out of the building.

It couldn't be a bomb threat, I thought, everyone was too relaxed. The teachers waved to one another, the children lined up alongside the bus driveway with excited smiles on their faces. After about ten minutes, a yellow school bus pulled into the parking lot. The waiting students immediately broke into loud, contagious applause, and when I saw the happy faces in the bus windows, I realized what we were doing—welcoming back the Green Valley students who had participated in the Special Olympics.

Everyone screamed and cheered as if the international Olympics were being held right before their eyes. The Special Olympians proudly descended from the school bus, medals atop their chests, their eyes aglow with joy. They waved and strutted as if they were world-famous heroes.

When we returned to the classroom, I cried from sheer joy. What a heavenly feeling those children gave me! *Lord*, I prayed, *those children are so lucky to have Vicki and her special kind of support.*

I felt that same kind of support from the cheering audience at the Miss Alabama Pageant. For the space of a few blessed hours, my exhaustion, hurt, and emotional pain were eased. That night was a gift from God, and the people of Alabama enriched my life more than I can describe.

Not too much later I appeared at the Special Olympics World Games. I was one of several celebrities scheduled to appear in the opening ceremonies. We were to rehearse in the afternoon and then go back to our hotels to eat and prepare for the actual events to be held that evening, but something went terribly wrong with the planners' schedules. Though we were supposed to rehearse for only fifteen minutes, we spent *four hours* waiting backstage with no end in sight.

We were all disgruntled, tired, and anxious, but one TV celebrity complained to the director and then lost his temper. "I'm not going to stay here a minute more," he said, waving his hands. "I've wasted four hours here for nothing." After exploding in frustration, he left for his hotel. I knew this wasn't just another celebrity temper tantrum. This individual was one of the kindest, nicest people I had met.

I didn't really blame him. It wasn't our fault that the schedule had gone awry, and it would have been nice to relax and prepare back at our hotel. But after the TV celebrity left, I heard people saying bad things about him. They called him names, they blasted his reputation with the ferocity they'd been directing at the program organizers only a few minutes before. They didn't consider that he had volunteered to appear, that he obviously believed in the Special Olympics or he wouldn't have even come, and that he had wasted four hours of his time.

Perfection's Pretty Hard to Please

I learned something through that experience. Most people expect celebrities to be perfect. Even in the midst of difficult circumstances, people will remember your one negative action or attitude even if you've done a hundred positive things.

What's the use? I wondered. *Why don't I just go home? I'm sick of the negative stories, the criticism, people who think I belong to them. I don't. Life is too short to live like this. . . .*

I had begun the year wanting to be remembered as a positive example of all a person with disabilities could accomplish, but I was only human. I had learned that I couldn't be perfect one hundred percent of the time. I had failed before, I would fail again, and I feared people would remember my failures more than my successes.

Like a car gasping on gasoline fumes, I was running on empty. And yet it was only July—my calendar was filled through the month of December with Miss America appearances and other scheduled speaking engagements. I wanted to rest. I remembered reading in the Bible that when Jesus needed rest, he sent the people away and hid himself on a mountain. I was ready to look for my own private hideaway as soon as my term of Miss America service was done, but friends warned me that I'd hurt my image if I canceled appearances I'd agreed to make as a former Miss America.

Numbly, I agreed to go on. Bonnie and Mickey encouraged me, and I discovered an inner discipline I didn't know I possessed. Maybe it was born during all those days of trying to make the proper sounds in my speech therapy, or maybe it was formed during all those endless pliés in ballet class. Ultimately, the strength that saw me through came from the spirit of God, who, though I hadn't made time for him, never once left my side.

You've probably seen Margaret Fishback Powers's poem "Footprints in the Sand" in which a man looks back over the path of his life and sees that God walked by his side until the times got rough. At those times, the man observes, he can see only one set of footprints. "Why?" he asks God, "why did you leave me during the hard times?"

God's answer is sure and strong. "I never left you," he assures the traveler. "When you see only one set of footprints, my child, those were the times I carried you."

During July and August, the last two months of my Miss America year, I was too tired to think. God was carrying me, still helping me make a difference, and I was too numb to even realize it. I was too tired to read my Bible, too tired to pray. But fortunately for me, the spirit of God helped in my distress. As Paul wrote: "For we don't even know what we should pray for, nor how we should pray. But the Holy Spirit prays for us with groanings that cannot be expressed in words. And the Father who knows all hearts knows what the Spirit is saying, for the

Spirit pleads for us believers in harmony with God's own will. And we know that God causes everything to work together for the good of those who love God and are called according to his purpose for them" (Romans 8:26–28).

I could do nothing but trust that God still had his hand on my life.

Later I was amazed to find that Helen Keller had dealt with the same exhaustion and pain I felt. In *Midstream* she wrote: "It is not true that I am never sad or rebellious; but long ago I determined not to complain. The mortally wounded must strive to live out their days cheerfully for the sake of others. That is what religion is for—to keep the hearts brave to fight it out to the end with a smiling face. This may not be a very lofty ambition, but it is a far cry from surrendering to fate. But to get the better of fate even to this extent one must have work and the solace of friendship and an unwavering faith in God's Plan of Good."[2]

I'd like to be able to tell you that my deafness never created a problem while I was Miss America, but I can't. Wearing the crown didn't suddenly make things easier, nor did it erase the difficulties I'd always striven to overcome. Receptions were difficult, as always. The buzzing from a room filled with talking people drove me to distraction after about fifteen minutes. I still found it difficult to read the lips of people with mustaches and/or thick accents. And when a sign language interpreter was present, people were still apt to say "Tell her I think she's great" without even looking in my direction.

Even after lots of practice, dealing with the national media was still a trying experience. The noise of a large press conference produced the same buzzing sounds I dreaded in receptions and airport terminals. For live interviews a sign language inter-

---

[2]Keller, *Midstream*, p. 261.

preter often stood right behind the television cameras, but I had to deal with a new interpreter every day. Each one signed a little differently, and few of them moved their lips as if they were speaking. I tried my best to see their sign language at the same time I read their lips, but it's hard to do both. When I was involved in a serious conversation with a reporter or broadcast journalist, I couldn't take the time to practice reading signs. And, as always, American Sign Language proved to be a barrier. The vocabulary is so basic that any difficult terms had to be finger-spelled, and I'd have to hesitate and literally watch the word forming letter by letter before my eyes.

I must have looked like a wide-eyed scatterbrain in interviews until I decided to ask that all televised conversations take place just between the reporter and me. Sometimes, especially in the glare of the bright television lights, I misunderstood the interviewer's question, but I figured it was better to be honest and admit my mistake than to sit with a vacant look on my face while someone spelled out the question.

Angels Unaware

During the times when I knew I'd made a mistake and wanted to quit, God sent someone to lift me up. Sometimes it was Bonnie or Mickey, sometimes it was someone I met along the Miss America journey. Often it was a hired driver of a hotel's limo or other car service.

I had a good rapport with drivers, and more than one of them brought interesting colors to my life. I think I liked talking to them because more than a few were immigrants who had come to the United States because they dreamed of a better life for their families. After a few months on the road as Miss America, I'd come to the conclusion that too many Americans take our country for granted. It was refreshing to talk to drivers and have my perspective adjusted.

Unfortunately, during those last few months I was so tired, I can't remember much of what I said to my driver friends. But a few months after I'd surrendered my title, I had to take the hotel limo for an hour's drive through the Virginia mountains to the airport. I was still tired and feeling very low, wondering whether or not I'd actually accomplished anything while I was Miss America. Life in the spotlight hadn't impressed me, and neither had most of the people who lived there.

The cabdriver seemed a refreshingly "normal" person, so I asked about his life. He told me that he had not graduated from high school. "But I don't regret anything," he assured me, glancing back in the rearview mirror. "I encouraged my children to graduate from high school and go to college, but I choose not to regret my life. If I do, my life will be nothing but miserable. So I look at the positive side of things. Here I am, working with a famous hotel! Every day I get to see trees, these beautiful mountains, this gorgeous view. I meet fascinating people who ride in my car, and they even pay me for the pleasure. Life is good!"

"You're so lucky!" I murmured, settling back against the seat. As Miss America, I had all too often been too tired to look at the positive side of things. I had forgotten the truth of one of my favorite Bible verses: "Trust in the Lord with all your heart; do not depend on your own understanding. Seek his will in all you do, and he will direct your paths" (Proverbs 3:5–6).

I was too apt to mourn the loss of my old life, but God hadn't really taken that life from me. Instead, he had led me to a different path, one that was part of my dream journey. The path I was now following was one my parents had never traveled, my friends had never traveled, not even other Miss Americas had traveled. I may have felt that I was walking this path alone, but I wasn't. God had promised to direct my path and stay with me as long as I sought his will in all I did, and trusted him with all my heart. Sometimes that seemed like a tall order, but then there were days like this one, when a warm and down-to-earth limo driver reminded me of what was important in life.

But there were other days when I wanted to pull my hair out. In Texas I was signing autographs at a shopping mall, when a woman walked up with a duck in her arms. She claimed the animal was deaf and wanted me to have my picture made with her duck. I could just see the headlines of the next day's paper: *Miss America Cries Fowl on Deaf Issues . . .*

Had I become a ridiculous figure? Was *anyone* taking my dream seriously?

A Crown Changes Things

I truly and deeply believe that God would have me honor my parents and my family. My parents and family worked hard to pursue life's best for me, and each of them made tremendous sacrifices in order to help me learn, live, and compete for the Miss America crown. I love each of them, and my sisters, grandparents, aunts, uncles, and cousins are the dearest people on earth to me. As a family, they have expended hundreds of hours to help me reach my goals, and I could never repay them for all they have done.

But no family is perfect, and mine had been severely shaken by divorce. When the added pressures of national attention, constant travel, a hectic schedule, and physical exhaustion were added to the strained relationship between the members of my family circle, something cracked.

During my pageant competitions I depended upon my family's support, but after I won the Miss America title, the situation changed. I no longer needed cheerleaders and helpers, because the Miss America office handled my affairs.

In the beginning of my Miss America year my mother and I appeared together at several functions. Since she had almost single-handedly engineered my educational experience, she spoke on acoupedics while I presented my STARS program. But after a while I wanted to discontinue the joint appearances. I was, after all, twenty-one years old, and I was ready to be independent. Furthermore, I didn't want people to see my mother and me together and assume that I needed her to communicate or function in the hearing world. I didn't. From the beginning she had raised me to be independent, and now I was ready to show the world how self-reliant a deaf woman could be.

I told my family how I felt and tried to prove that I hadn't changed, but I had no control over many aspects of my life. I realized with startling clarity that my old life was gone for good. Even if I quit, things would never be the same. I'd always have to deal with people wanting autographs, students writing to interview me for their school assignments, girls wanting advice about how to compete in the pageant system. . . .

When Miss America 1997 was to appear on *The Tonight Show with Jay Leno*, in his opening monologue Jay mentioned that once you're Miss America, you're always Miss America. "It's like the Mafia," he joked. "You can try to get away, but they just keep pulling you back in." The joke fell flat with the TV audience, but I understood the grim humor behind it. Once that crown is placed on your head, there's no getting away from it.

I certainly couldn't seem to get away from it, no matter how much I wanted to. The crown meant one thing to me, and something different to my friends, family, and the rest of the world.

In my exhaustion, the crown was becoming a burden. Toward the end of my term of service I kept thinking, "Maybe I just won't eat. Who'll care if I starve?" But a voice inside told me that I would greatly disappoint God if I took my own life. There were times when I wept and begged God to take my life away. Now I can't believe that I would make such a request to the powerful God of the universe. I must have seemed so ungrateful for all the things he had done for me, but my thoughts were centered on my problems.

Though part of me wanted to die, I can honestly say that I never tried to kill myself. That would have been an affront to God. I just felt that life wasn't worth living. I had Bonnie or Mickey and Jesus with me always, but I wasn't looking at Jesus, and Bonnie and Mickey couldn't fill the hole in my heart.

As I traveled around the country, I heard criticism not even Bonnie and Mickey heard. When I stood in front of an auditorium and listened to the applause of an audience, I couldn't hear the compliments people spoke, but I could read the sign language of the deaf people present. More than once I saw someone signing, "She's stupid, she always talks" and "She never understands deaf people." More than once I stood and tried to smile as my cheeks burned after reading what some deaf people were saying about me. At that moment I could have been handed a hundred warm and supportive letters from deaf people and hearing people like Donna Dickman of the Alexander Graham Bell Association for the Deaf, but it wouldn't have mattered. I wasn't following my own advice about being positive; I was allowing my own negative attitude to color my perceptions.

I tried to ignore those critical comments, but as they persisted throughout the year, I became more and more discouraged. My hope was dying. I wanted to make a positive difference for deaf people, I wanted to help children, and yet I couldn't see that I had accomplished anything.

I had been doing the same thing, making the same speech, meeting strangers day after day, telling the same stories, the same jokes, answering the same questions, signing the same name over and over again. I felt so recycled that I didn't know who Heather Whitestone was anymore. I was uncertain about the future, and didn't know how I'd handle the Miss America burden for the rest of my life. I was tired of hearing the word "disability" as if it defined who I was. I was trying to make others see the deaf and blind as people first, but instead of supporting me, some people greeted my work with a chorus of complaint.

Then one day, on a long flight, I opened my Bible. I'd taken it out of my suitcase as an act of desperation; I knew I needed something to help me finish the year or I wouldn't make it. I didn't really know where to turn, so I opened to the Song of Solomon and began to read. I had no idea what this book was about, but I felt strangely led to read this section of the Bible.

I'll never understand the power contained in the word of God. The Song of Solomon is a love poem, and that selection somehow made me feel normal again. Reading about God's love filled me with the strength I needed to survive. God's love literally saved my despairing heart in those moments, and I recalled my favorite verse, Jeremiah 17:7–8: "But blessed are those who trust in the Lord and have made the Lord their hope and confidence. They are like trees planted along a riverbank, with roots that reach deep into the water. Such trees are not bothered by the heat or worried by long months of drought. Their leaves stay green, and they go right on producing delicious fruit."

I couldn't see the larger picture then, and I couldn't understand all that God wanted to do in my life. But I listened with my heart, and I heard God's voice. He did care. He had not left me alone. And if I would trust in him, he would continue to guide me along the path where he had placed me. We had begun this journey together, not on that Atlantic City runway, but back in my room when I had asked Jesus to be my savior. He had never left me—but I had taken my focus off him.

I was, God assured me, just like a tree planted by a river-bank, but I'd taken my eyes off the source of the living water to stare instead at the boulders in the river. I'd allowed myself to become angry, worried, and fretful about obstacles that didn't have to concern me.

God was my source. He would sustain me no matter how many hulking boulders appeared in that rushing river.

All I had to do was trust.

8 A New Beginning

As I walked down the Atlantic City runway after being crowned Miss America, I wanted to tell the world that Jesus had helped me shape and achieve my dreams according to God's will.

But I never thought I would go through so many battles during my year of service. In the beginning I tried to talk about Jesus because I wanted to spread the good news about him through the national media, but being a witness was difficult. All too often reporters were interested only in dramatic stories or conflicts, the more negative, the better. Most of them didn't want to hear about my personal faith or the practical ways God had worked in my life and set me on this journey to my dream.

At one press conference a reporter asked about the Americans with Disabilities Act. Would it, he asked, help a disabled individual find a job?

My answer was simple: "If God wants it to happen, it will happen. If God wants a particular person with disabilities to have an opportunity, he will change others' attitudes and send that opportunity."

The reporters just stared at me with disbelieving looks on their faces. I knew they thought I was either brainwashed or as naïve as a child, but it didn't matter. I have never tried to hide the fact that I am a Christian. I could do nothing apart from God's help and guiding hand.

In the beginning of my year I routinely signed my autograph and then added a reference to a Bible verse under my name and title. Sometimes people would look at what I'd written and then hand the autograph back, asking for another one. Other times they weren't bold enough to hand it back, but I could see from their facial expressions that they weren't happy to see the Bible verse included. I thought it was sad that they should have such a negative perspective of Christians.

At one of my pageants the judges asked how I wanted to be remembered after the pageant. "Without a doubt," I answered, "I want you to remember Jesus in me."

When I began my Miss America year I wanted to change the world and influence people in a powerful way. I dreamed that through the early detection program all pediatricians would decide to routinely give hearing tests to babies; I had great hopes for my work with the President's Committee on the Employment of People with Disabilities. And I wanted everyone to know that Jesus was my savior and that God had brought me to this place as I followed the dream he had given me. I wanted to be like a keg of dynamite that would explode and set the world on fire for good things.

I waited—there was no explosion. I couldn't see that any of my goals were being realized.

But then I was reminded of something Mother Teresa once said: "We can do no great things—only small things with great love."

I've always loved and admired Mother Teresa. I remember once watching her on Robert Schuller's *Hour of Power*. The Reverend Schuller asked Mother Teresa, "Where does peace come from?" and she answered, "It comes from your smile." In her smile I saw great love. She touched my heart in a profound way.

I am certain that Mother Teresa dreamed of world peace and conquering poverty in many countries. I am also certain she knew she could never accomplish these goals; only God could work such a miracle. But still she continued her work, greeting orphan children, changing their diapers, feeding hungry men. One soul at a time, one heart at a time, she gave them her smile . . . and her love.

Atlantic City Again

As I flew to Atlantic City to formally end my term as Miss America, I thought about the thousands of people I had met during the past months. Though I had often been tired, I had at least given them a smile. I may not have been all I wanted to be or accomplished all I set out to do, but I tried to do my best. I am sure there were times when I forced myself to smile even when I did not want to. I know there were times when people sensed I was not in a good mood. But most of the time God gave me the strength to share his love with the people I met.

Parents of small children with hearing impairment were constantly telling me how I gave them hope simply by winning the title "Miss America." They watched my actions carefully, and I knew they had monitored my reactions to criticism from part of the deaf community. I still believed the only way to win people's hearts was to love, not retaliate. I want my deaf friends to see the positive aspects of themselves. They can listen to their hearts and follow their dreams . . . and I hope they will.

My pensive mood lifted as I remembered two of the most special days of my entire year. The first was the day John Healy of Chicago invited me to his house to share peanut butter and jelly sandwiches with his wife and five adorable children. I had been complaining about the endless stream of banquet food (mostly chicken and/or shrimp, green beans, and mashed potatoes in every conceivable shape), and John said, "Why don't you come to my house? I think we can rustle up a little peanut butter and jelly."

We did, and that was the best meal I ate that entire year! Chunky peanut butter and luscious strawberry jelly on soft white bread, served in a real kitchen with children and noise and a ringing telephone . . . that sandwich tasted like *home*.

My second unforgettable day was one I spent with Carlene Weachock, who works in public relations for Waterford crystal. Carlene reminded me of my athletic sister, Melissa—she has blond hair and a natural beauty that doesn't require a lot of makeup. I always loved doing appearances for Waterford because Carlene would be there, and I always felt at home with her.

As children, Melissa and I often rode our bikes in our neighborhood and the nearby woods. I always felt incredibly alive when I could smell the fresh air and see the trees and sky. As a child, I was always busy in the house, working on my speech or my homework, so when Melissa took me on a bike ride, she seemed like an angel taking me out for a little taste of heaven.

Carlene did the same thing one day in Florida. I had been spending all my time breathing the stale air of airports, airplanes, and hotels, and in between flights I'd done nothing but speak about my STARS platform. Carlene met us in Florida, where we were scheduled to do an appearance with the gentleman who made the crystal Miss America scepter. But instead of spending our spare time at a hotel, Carlene surprised us and took Mickey and me to a little island near Tampa, where she rented three bicycles. We rode around the island on a beautiful cloudy day, then found ourselves in the middle of an honest-to-goodness downpour. We laughed and pedaled faster, then biked under the shelter of a group of trees to wait out the storm.

My heart was about to burst with joy as I watched Carlene and Mickey pumping their bikes toward that tree. I was so lucky—so *blessed*—to have friends who would stop for a moment to enjoy life with me. I had received hundreds of letters from people thanking me for serving as an example to them—something I hadn't consciously been aware of doing—and I appreciated these people who had sacrificially given of themselves to bring me the gift of laughter.

Miss America Beauty

Though the Miss America Organization has worked hard to emphasize that the competition is first and foremost a scholarship pageant, in the minds of many people it will always be a beauty pageant. Quite often during my term of service I fielded questions from teen magazines on my "beauty routine" (drink water, exercise, and sleep when you can!) and "healthy diet" (I had to eat whatever was placed before me on the banquet table!). On my rare days off I'd slip into blue jeans and a T-shirt and sit around the hotel room without makeup. I'm sure the bellboys who brought in my room service trays had no idea they were serving Miss America!

Like most girls, in high school I felt the usual pressure to be "beautiful." I suppose it's part of being an adolescent—

teenage girls want to be pretty enough to attract attention from the boys; beauty and popularity seem to go hand in hand. But as I sat in my bedroom, reading my Bible, I discovered that God's definition of beauty is a lot different from the world's. God says that beauty is found in a gentle, quiet, and obedient spirit.

As a teenager, I wasn't quite sure God knew what he was talking about! My parents and I were having some major disagreements in those days, and I didn't want to be gentle, quiet, or obedient! I knew that God had placed me with my parents for his reasons, but I didn't want to dwell on that truth. Though God had used my parents to put me in dance class when I was little, and though by high school I knew that God wanted me to do something for him through ballet, my mother wasn't cooperating! I wanted to join the Ballet Magnificat, the Christian ballet company, and my mother disapproved! How could she? How could obeying her—quietly and gently—be part of God's will, when it was so *obvious* that I belonged in that Christian ballet troupe?

I couldn't see the logic in obeying my parents, but as I searched the Scriptures I couldn't find any way around obedience. God didn't say, "Obey your parents *unless* they want you to do something you don't want to do." He said *obey*. And so I did, because I trusted God.

I thought God had goofed up when my mother didn't want me to join the Ballet Magnificat; then she steered me toward Jacksonville State University, which had no ballet class. *Whoa,* I thought, after realizing that I wouldn't be able to dance for nearly a full year, *this can't be God's will! I'm supposed to serve him through my dance, but how can I stay in shape and be a fit servant if I'm out of practice?*

Then God spoke to my heart, and I listened: *Obey. Trust me. And continue to honor your parents' wishes.* My parents hadn't *commanded* me to attend JSU, but I knew it was clearly their preference. And so, despite my strong desire to dance, I obeyed again.

All through JSU, even through my pageant experiences, God kept telling me that he would work through my dance. Not only would he do something, but he was going to do something *big*. I didn't know if his plans included winning Miss Alabama or Miss America, but lately I've come to see that the scope of God's dream for me was far wider than I had imagined. As I write, it has been two full years since I surrendered the Miss America title, and when I attended the 1997 pageant, people were still coming up and telling me how much they had appreciated my "Via Dolorosa" ballet. How can I judge the effect of those two and a half minutes? I cannot know how it touched the hearts of the millions who saw it, at least not on this side of eternity. But God, in his infinite power, can take my simple dance and multiply its influence just as Jesus multiplied that little boy's humble loaves and fishes to feed the five thousand.

Because I listened to my heart and obeyed my parents' wishes, in his timing God led me to win one pageant, then another, and finally Miss America. And when I had reached the end of my ability to cope, God revealed himself as my strength and the love of my heart.

And that's where true beauty is found—in the heart. God showed me that when we obey his principles and treat other people with love, that's the most beautiful thing he's ever seen. God measures my beauty by how I touch other people's lives, by how I demonstrate his love to them.

I've met so many lovely girls over the years. Some of them are so beautiful, they've always had everything they wanted. Life seems easy for them. I remember talking to one girl and thinking that she didn't understand life at all. Her life had been nothing but parties, fun, and gossip. I don't think she had suffered or been lonely a single day in her life.

During my high school years, I honestly thought I was ugly. Only a few guys asked me out, I wasn't popular and outgoing, I didn't win homecoming queen or Shelby County Junior Miss. But as I began to study God's word, I found that by being loving, gentle, and kind, I could win people's hearts.

During my term of service I met a lovely woman who was kind enough to interview me for a television show. The interview went well, but during every commercial break she'd pick up a hand mirror, fix her hair, or call her makeup person over for a quick touch-up. Once she leaned over to me and asked, "And what do you use for those tiny little wrinkles around the eyes?"

I laughed. "I'm just twenty-one," I told her. "I'm not worried about wrinkles yet!" To tell you the truth, I don't think I'll worry much about them when I'm forty. To me, wrinkles are beautiful. They symbolize gentleness in the same way the Bible says gray hair is a symbol of wisdom. Too many people think that youth equals success. It doesn't.

As I began to pull my energies together to face the end of my year as Miss America, I fed myself positive words, the best beauty formula I know. And I reminded myself of the advice I'd given another girl who had come off the stage during a pageant competition and promptly thrown a fit.

"What's wrong?" I had asked her.

"I didn't walk right," she said, her bottom lip edging forward in a pout. She crossed her arms. "I didn't walk the way I was supposed to."

I looked her straight in the eye. "Let me give you some advice. If you're looking for a beauty job, go take pictures for a modeling agency or compete in the Miss USA pageant. This is a scholarship pageant, and the judges are more interested in your heart than in your looks. Don't worry about how you walked—worry about whether or not the judges saw your heart."

As the jet descended into Atlantic City, I could only hope that America had seen my heart in the past year. I had tried to smile and show God's love. Now it was time to leave the Miss America stage and continue on the path God had laid out for me.

Pageant Week

Bert Parks used to joke that Miss America contestants live like the army during pageant week—that they have to tell their hostess where they're going every minute of the day. That's not too far from the truth, because the contestants are guarded for security reasons, but the Miss America hostesses are so sweet and nice, I never really minded being accountable to them.

My mother and father came up for my final pageant, also Dad's wife, Terri; Melissa and her daughter, Sarah; Aunt Stephanie; Aunt Gloria; Grandmother Whitestone; Granddaddy and Grandmother Gray; and my cousin Trey.

I was a little nervous about participating in this pageant. The Miss America board had asked me to dance again, but they wanted me to dance with men, and I'd never danced on-stage with a partner in my entire life. Two weeks before the televised pageant, we began rehearsals in Birmingham, and my dance teacher, Monica, found a man to stand in for the men I'd work with in Atlantic City. Unfortunately, during one of those rehearsals, he accidentally caught me too tightly during a lift. I suffered a huge bruise on my rib (which wasn't broken, thank goodness), and the doctor told me not to dance for five days. That didn't leave much time to practice before the pageant!

Things didn't go much better during rehearsals in Atlantic City. While still wearing a big bandage around my waist, I practiced with male dancers I'd never even met. Something went wrong during the preliminary pageant every night—one night I twisted my ankle, another night my partner almost dropped me, another night I was far behind the music. I was really beginning to get nervous. The sponsors had spent millions and millions of dollars on this program, and I wanted to do my part to make it a success. And this was the seventy-fifth anniversary of the pageant, so the Miss America officials had a lot invested in this special production. Forty-one former Miss Americas had agreed to participate in the pageant, more than had ever returned to Atlantic City at one time.

As the night of the pageant approached, I found that I was more concerned about the dance than about surrendering my title. I was happy to pass on the responsibilities and the hectic travel schedule. But I felt a huge responsibility to the sponsors, the Miss America office, and all the people who would be watching on television. The feeling that gripped me as I dressed in my dance costume and tied up my toe shoes was completely different from the one I'd experienced the year before when God said, "Relax and dance for me."

Despite my nervousness and my shaking legs, everything went smoothly. The old stage maxim of "bad rehearsal, good performance" rang true, because the dance came off without a hitch. People said afterward that it looked like I'd been dancing with partners for ages. The next year, when I visited the 1997 Miss America Pageant, choreographer Anita Mann told me that she and Charone Mose had earned an Emmy for best choreography for their work on the 1996 Miss America Pageant. For that, I can only thank God.

When the dance was over, I went back to the dressing room and cried for five minutes, caught up in sheer nervousness.

Then I touched up my makeup, slipped into my evening gown, and prepared for my final walk down the runway.

A chapter was about to close, but the book was far from finished. As I walked out on the runway to say good-bye to the crowd, I was mentally ready to go home and resume my normal life. I paused at the end of the runway, recalling how just a year before I had heard God assuring me that he would go with me every step of the way. *Thank you, Father.* I breathed a prayer. *It's over.*

My heart stilled when I heard the voice of God again speaking to my heart: *It's not over. I'm not finished with you yet.*

Why not? I turned and began my walk back to the stage, eager to surrender my title. What could God possibly have for me to do now? And why couldn't he use someone else? I was tired, I was emotionally drained, I wasn't a fit instrument for anything. . . .

I pushed those thoughts aside as the pageant continued. Maybe I'd misunderstood. After all, what new opportunities could possibly appear? I'd done just about everything as Miss America.

And so I watched the rest of the pageant with mingled joy and relief. But a friend of mine had warned me that I might soon experience different feelings about the end of my Miss America year:

> *I know sooner or later you are going to be sad that it is all over. Remember, being sad and missing something is a natural feeling. I will be there to lend you a shoulder to cry on. Focus on how incredible this past year has been. It has been a blessing to you and so many other people. Throughout your life, you've made so many sacrifices in order to obey the dream that God gave you. As a result of your faithfulness, look at all the blessings God has showered on you. The exciting part of this whole adventure is that it has only begun.*

At my graduation, the speaker said that commencement addresses are a beginning. You are graduating from Miss America. You may be sad, but you will have countless memories to take with you. You will belong to a sorority of women with only seventy-five members. While the transition from the old world of Miss America to a new world may be difficult, God will be with you every step of the way, waiting for you to ask for divine guidance, and I will be there as your loving friend.

I wish you the best on your new journey.

John McCallum

Little did I know how much I would need that shoulder to cry on . . . or just how loving I would find that friend. And as I sighed in relief and crowned Shawntel Smith Miss America 1996, if you had told me that in less than ten months I would be Heather Whitestone McCallum, I'd have laughed aloud.

But I was.

9 An Engaging Secret

"Do you have a boyfriend?"

The sweet, freckle-faced little girl shyly asked the question.

"No, there's no one special," I answered, smiling back at her. I knew young girls like her looked up to Miss America, and I didn't want them to think that if Miss America had a boyfriend, they needed to find one too. I wanted them to know that it's okay not to have a boyfriend. "God has a unique dream for you," I told them, "and you don't need a boyfriend to feel special. You *are* special, and you need to appreciate yourself before you can love others."

But as my year drew to a close, I was dating John McCallum as often as I could, which wasn't very often! We weren't "going steady." In fact, I had asked John how he felt about me dating other men as well. To my surprise, he answered, "I don't have time to worry. If you want to date other men, that's between you and God. I trust God completely, and I trust you. If we are meant to become serious, God will show us when the time is right."

I wasn't ready for a serious commitment; in fact, I'd been so influenced by the "get your education, establish a career" mind-set that I couldn't really see myself getting married before I was twenty-seven or twenty-eight. Most people today wait until they're older to marry, but they feel free to live together. I was committed to chastity, so I knew a live-in relationship wasn't an option for me. But my friends continued to urge me to graduate from college and accomplish my dreams before marriage.

What were my dreams at that point? My greatest dream was to make a positive difference in other people's lives, and why couldn't I do that as a married woman?

I had first met John McCallum in the waiting room outside Newt Gingrich's office in March 1995. John was working as an aide for Newt, and while I spent forty minutes waiting, we made polite small talk. He had such a youthful face, I found it hard to believe he was old enough to work in a congressional office! When Newt was finally able to see me, Mickey and I went in, took a picture, thanked him for his support for the President's Committee on Employment of People with Disabilities, and left.

Not long afterward, I received a letter from John on congressional letterhead. After recognizing the stationery, the Miss America office gave the letter to Bonnie, and she brought it with her when she joined me.

"Heather," she said, waving the letter in front of my eyes. "You've got a date!"

I was sitting at the table, working on an upcoming speech; I didn't want to think about dates. "Yeah, right," I murmured.

"I'm serious," Bonnie went on. "It's a letter from that young man you met in Newt's office."

Bonnie read the letter to me. John asked for an autographed picture (everyone does!) and then said, "If you are ever in Washington or the surrounding area, I would be honored to escort you to dinner. God knows there must be times when you want to get away from always being Miss America. I'm sure that can be stressful. I'm a fine and honorable Christian man and it would be a pleasure to give you the VIP tour of Washington, D.C. I hope you are not offended by my request. If so, please accept my apology."

Bonnie was a lot more excited than I was. "He sounds wonderful!" she said, enthusiastically waving the letter at me. "Call him, Heather!"

"Bonnie," I said in as serious a voice as I could manage. "I don't have time to date anyone. I'm too busy. I have a job to do." In the letter John had included a copy of the picture Newt's office staff had taken with me. "Besides," I went on, figuring out which man he was, "that guy has a baby face. He's probably younger than I am."

"Come on, he works for Newt," Bonnie urged. "And he says he's a Christian."

"He just said it because he thinks I want to hear it."

"Heather." Now it was Bonnie's turn to be serious. "Let me tell you something. I have traveled with Miss Americas for six years, and I've learned that men are chicken. But this one has guts. Because men are so frightened away by the title 'Miss America,' you're going to have only a few opportunities to date. This is one of them. If I were you, I'd take it!"

I sighed and looked up at her. If I didn't accept this guy's invitation, I'd never hear the end of it. "Okay, for you, Bonnie, I'll do it."

"Good." Bonnie beamed. "You've got to have fun, Heather, you're too serious all the time." She moved toward the telephone. "You need a life, you need to have fun."

Bonnie called John's office and got his answering machine. I pretended not to listen as she spoke—loudly—into the telephone: "This is Bonnie Sirgany, Miss America's traveling companion. Heather received your letter and would *love* to go out with you. We'll give you another call when we come back to Washington."

"Bonnie," I said after she'd hung up. "You didn't have to say I'd *love* to go out with him. You make it sound like I'm looking for a relationship. You could have just said I'd be interested in having dinner."

Bonnie just laughed.

We went back to Washington twice after that, and each time John turned down my offer of a date. The first time he was traveling to California on business, the second time he said he had to attend a friend's wedding. I didn't take his cancellations personally; I really wasn't interested and didn't care. But Bonnie was determined that Miss America should have A Date, and she persisted. Finally, on Bonnie's third attempt to set something up, John said he was available.

Miss America 1995 would have her first date.

Unfortunately, Bonnie wasn't there to see it. She and Mickey had switched places, but I think Mickey was as excited about this development as Bonnie was. John called Mickey to work out the details. When he asked if I needed any sort of security, Mickey purred, "All she needs is you!"

The Date

John took me to the romantic Hotel Washington rooftop restaurant that overlooks the back lawn of the White House. When our appetizers arrived, John bowed his head to thank the Lord for the food.

I was glad he bowed his head, because I didn't want him to
see the look of skepticism that crossed my face as I read his
lips. Was he really a Christian, or was this prayer just for show?
A lot of people knew about my faith because of my dance to
"Via Dolorosa." I knew that sometimes men will try to impress
a woman, so when John lifted his head, I leaned forward and
let him have it with both barrels: "Tell me how you became a
Christian."

John's brown eyes widened. "Okay," he said, gulping hard.
And then he proceeded to tell me about the time he had
prayed and asked Jesus Christ to be his savior.

If he had told me that he went to church regularly or that
he gave faithfully to the Red Cross, I'd have yawned and gone
back to the hotel, pleading a headache. I didn't have time to
spend on meaningless relationships. But John gave me an honest and sincere answer, so I stayed. For fifteen minutes he told
me about his salvation experience, and then—finally—we finally began to eat. I had wanted to hear only a short story, not
a novel! I was starving!

After the appetizers we visited yet another restaurant, the
Red Sage, and enjoyed a nice dinner. But near the end of the
meal John excused himself from the table. I waited alone for
several minutes, then began to wonder where in the world he
had gone.

So many thoughts ran through my brain! Maybe I'd embarrassed him somehow, and he didn't want to go through the
scene of returning me to my hotel. Or maybe I'd scared him
when I demanded to know the history and basis of his faith.
Or maybe he was off in a corner somewhere, collecting on a
bet he'd made with his buddies: "Yeah, sure I can get Miss
America to go out with me."

I began to be uncomfortably aware that I was a woman sitting alone at a table, and people were watching me (or at least

it felt like they were). In order to have something to do, I pulled a pen from my purse and began to doodle on a sheet of paper. I drew a picture of a tree and grass, but still there was no sign of John. I hadn't been left alone for more than a few moments in an entire year, and a wave of apprehension swept through me. What if he didn't come back?

I drew a house. No John. I drew windows and a chimney, but John didn't appear. I drew birds, drank iced tea, and flagged down a busboy just to have someone to talk to. My fear veered to anger as the moments crept by, and by the time John finally returned to the table, I was politely furious.

"What took you so long?"

"Don't worry," he said, smiling as he brushed my question aside. "Nothing to worry about."

Had he been in the rest room? Was he sick? He didn't say, and it occurred to me that he might be too embarrassed to volunteer an explanation. I left the matter alone.

When he escorted me back to the hotel, he turned and said, "I'd love to take you out again. Is that okay with you?"

From out of nowhere my answer came: "Sure!" I don't know why I said that, I certainly wasn't feeling inclined to give him another opportunity to abandon me in a restaurant.

Mickey waited up to hear all the details. "It was a normal night," I told her, shrugging. "But he stayed in the rest room a long time."

"Heather," Mickey said, fixing me in a stern glance. "You scared him to death."

"Did not. I didn't do anything."

"Heather, I know you. You're so outspoken, you scare people sometimes."

That's when I saw the note someone had slipped under the door. I picked it up and opened the envelope:

Dear Heather:

I knew I was going to have a wonderful evening so I took some time to write this short note.

First, let me say thanks for calling me back. It's every little boy's dream to meet Miss America. Also, thank you for your kind letter and the autographed picture. It's funny, I think I knew you were a Christian before I met you. You have set such a wonderful example for all Americans who have faced adversity in their lives, and you have proven that a disability can be a blessing in disguise. You have truly proven that the Lord works in mysterious ways.

Thanks for such a wonderful evening. I hope you will keep in touch.

Sincerely,
John McCallum

The second half of the note had been written in a different color ink. Two or three days later, when I spoke to John on the phone, I asked why he'd taken so long in the rest room.

"The rest room?" he asked, laughing. "I wasn't in the rest room. I was sitting at another table, trying to finish that note for you."

A Sorely Needed Friend

John gave me something new to think about as I finished up my term of service. Helen Keller had written that her friend Samuel Clemens always made her feel like a human being. "He knew that we do not think with eyes and ears," she wrote, "and that our capacity for thought is not measured by five senses. He kept me always in mind while he talked, and he treated me like a competent human being. That is why I loved him. . . ."[1]

---

[1] Keller, *Midstream*, p. 66.

I felt the same way about John. So many men I met during my Miss America year talked about disabilities, and those conversations only made me feel . . . *disabled*. Did they think I always wanted to talk about disability issues? I'm a person first! John saw that, and he never mentioned my deafness. He knew I loved nature, so we talked about the outdoors, we talked about God and Jesus, we talked about politics and government. He made me feel like a human being, not a deaf person. He treated me as he would have treated any girl, and I appreciated that.

I feel the same things everyone else feels. My deafness is not an essential part of my existence; sometimes I don't feel at all handicapped. I live in the real world, and all of its fullness is available for me to enjoy.

After that first date, John became a true friend. He supported me through those difficult last months with regular phone calls and faxes. I can't imagine our courtship without a fax machine! He obviously put a lot of time and thought into his encouraging messages, and they never failed to inspire and encourage me.

John came to Philadelphia to surprise me on what became our third date. He had received my itinerary, so he knew where we'd be. I walked out of the airplane, then turned and saw him standing there, a bouquet of flowers in his hands. In his blue jacket, pale pants, and preppy shoes, he looked like a politician . . . and if he was hoping to get a hug, he was disappointed.

Bonnie was excited to see him, she gave him a big hug while I stood beside her and tried to hide my jealousy. I really liked him, politician or not, but I didn't want to show my feelings. I had to make sure he liked Heather Whitestone and was not some young man infatuated with the idea of dating Miss America.

Later, another time when John met us at the airport, he stood at the gate with a sign like the ones limo drivers routinely hold up to identify themselves to people they're supposed to meet. John's sign simply said BIG HUG. That time I laughed and gave him the hug he wanted.

As my job became more strenuous and difficult, I began to thank God for sending John my way. I was so strong at the beginning of my Miss America year. I was full of energy, faith, and hope, ready to influence the world with my heart and the crown. But as time went on, I collapsed. I had been determined to try to find time to study God's word again, but I'd become so discouraged and exhausted, it was far easier to come back to my hotel every day and fall into bed. I couldn't do it by myself.

And that's when God brought John into my life.

John had an incredible heart for God, and I knew that to continue to make a positive difference, I needed the strength John could provide. In Ecclesiastes 4 I read: "Two people can accomplish more than twice as much as one; they get a better return for their labor. If one person falls, the other can reach out and help. But people who are alone when they fall are in real trouble."

We weren't seriously considering marriage, but I grew to depend upon John's friendship. I knew he was vitally interested in politics—a business I had come to distrust and dislike—and I couldn't see myself as a statesman's wife. And so we continued to keep in touch by phone and fax and the occasional date when our paths crossed. And for the first six months of our friendship, our relationship was as platonic as that between a brother and sister.

I found it difficult to believe that John could be falling in love with me. I wasn't at my best during those last months as Miss America, and I frequently let my frustrations fly when I was with John. Once we had a minor argument, and I thought the friendship was finished. But John stayed by my side and forgave my outburst. I was bitter and angry and tired, but he said none of those things prevented him from seeing Jesus in my heart.

I was amazed when he forgave me so easily. I thought that love had to be proven over a long period of time, and yet he made no demands on me, he simply forgave me. I was stunned. I had kept him at arm's length for months, being a friend but no more, keeping my heart and my emotions safely out of reach. I didn't want to risk too much—what if he suddenly lost interest after my last walk on that Atlantic City runway?

And then he wrote and said, "I am falling in love with you." And that admission took my breath away. I didn't know whether to be excited or shocked. My heart filled with joy, but I didn't know if it was the right feeling or not. I was grateful that God had sent a fine Christian man my way, but I hadn't told John the extent of my feelings. I missed him terribly and wanted to see him, but didn't dare tell him how much I cared.

"Come to Atlantic City," I told him on the phone. "You'll enjoy the pageant. I don't know how much time I'll be able to spend with you, but I think you'll have a good time. And I know I'll be happy to know you're in the audience. I could really use your support as I dance again."

So John came to Atlantic City. We didn't spend much time together, in fact, only my family members and the Miss America officials even knew that John was a special person in my life. We still weren't serious about a future together, but just knowing he was there meant a lot to me.

After I surrendered my title, I didn't travel through Washington, D.C., as often, so we saw less of each other. John told me he was thinking about moving to Atlanta, because he knew I would be in Birmingham more often and it'd be easier to commute from Birmingham to Atlanta than from Washington. I agreed.

And then the storm clouds began to gather.

The Ultimatum

The month after I became Heather Whitestone, private citizen, I went to Washington, D.C., to speak at a convention designed to acquaint our congressmen with deaf issues. The convention organizers had gone through a lot of trouble to set up displays, organize the schedule, purchase billboards, provide interpreters, and so on. I worked hard on my speech and did my best to look and sound professional. The organizers sent invitations to every senator and representative, and I looked forward to speaking about the benefits of an early hearing loss detection program.

I was very impressed by the size and scope of that convention. There were many speakers on the program—doctors, a former professional baseball player with a hearing loss, a famous deaf comedian, and other professionals—and we had all been told to limit our remarks to five minutes because the congressional representatives had busy schedules. I was ready and eager to share, but was sharply disappointed when it became obvious that few people in Washington cared enough to do more than put in token appearances.

Some representatives came, stayed five minutes, looked around, then left. One sent a staff member to represent him. The vast majority never even showed up. I lost most of the respect I held for politicians in general, and considered it a waste of time to even go through the motions of speaking to Congress. None of the people we were trying to reach were listening, and everyone at that meeting knew it.

I was still furious when I went to my next engagement in North Carolina. During a free hour I picked up the phone and bluntly told John: "Look, I know you dream of serving in government, but, John, those people—well, they stink. I don't know how you can serve God alongside people like that. I don't think you should get involved in politics at all."

When I paused from my tirade to catch a breath, I heard dead silence on the phone. John wasn't agreeing with me—he wasn't saying anything. I felt a sudden wave of crazy, erratic fear. Without even realizing it, I had given him an ultimatum: your dream or me.

"If you can't support my dream," John said finally, his voice flat and matter-of-fact, "then I can't see you anymore. I don't want a woman—any woman—to take away the dream God has given me."

I didn't know what to do. My thoughts had been slowly turning toward marriage, and I'd been trying to imagine myself as a statesman's wife. But how could I be a politician's wife if I had no respect for politicians? I felt that most of them didn't care, they didn't respect other people's work. I'd just seen evidence of that in Washington. . . .

Theresa Hawkins, the young lady who was serving as my companion now that I was traveling on my own, saw my tears and tactfully suggested a walk along the beach. Numbly, I followed her outside, and for a long time we walked, not saying anything.

I know God gave Theresa the words to say. As we walked, she bent suddenly and picked up a black stone and a broken shell from the water's edge. "Do you see this rock?" she said, holding it out on her palm. "And this broken shell? Look at the waves, Heather. Imagine the waves crashing down on you all the time. The shell is broken because it is weak, but this stone is strong, and the waves couldn't break it. Instead, they've polished it, leaving it smooth and shiny. Unlike the shell, the rock has no rough edges."

The truth of her analogy hit me like a bolt from the blue.

The broken shell was like a person who did not have Jesus, but the stone represented someone like me, like John, for Jesus himself said, "I am the Rock." The stone could bring beauty and joy to others because it had allowed itself to be pummeled, polished, and cast upon the shore. To be *used* in whatever way God saw fit. That rock belonged to God. It had no right to demand its own way, and neither did I.

That night I called John and apologized. I told him about the rock, and as I spoke I knew that God was calling me to marry him. And I realized that when a couple has a major disagreement, that disagreement will either be the making or the breaking of them. When I begged for John's forgiveness, he said he needed time to think things over.

I felt terrible. For a year I had publicly touted the importance of following God-given dreams, and John had confided in me about his—and then, in a moment of fury, I'd said, "Forget that dream. Those people hurt my feelings." Like a spoiled princess I had tried to control John, I had even tried to control God's plan for John.

Later that night I prayed and asked God to forgive me too. My strong will and stubborn streak had again reared its ugly head.

We didn't see each other for several days. In that time of silence I realized that John was the man I needed, the man God had sent me. But I had to trust, and I had to be patient. When John finally did call me back to settle things between us, our love immediately deepened. We moved from the foothills of friendship to the mountain of commitment.

We knew our love would have to stand the tests of time and distance, but we placed our trust and faith in God. John told me, "I am not going to give up on you just because things might be difficult. I love overcoming obstacles. I love depending on God for my success."

The Proposal

In November, just two months after I surrendered my title, John and I were together again in Washington, D.C. I had flown up to do some work with a speaker's bureau, and John picked me up at my hotel. Before we went to dinner, John suggested that we swing by Newt Gingrich's office so he could pick up some "homework."

"I didn't know you had homework," I said, laughing. I went with him to Newt's office, then followed him to the balcony of the Capitol building. We could see the Washington Monument from where we stood, and a bright moon had begun to climb the sky.

"John, you lied to me," I teased him, a sneaking suspicion forming in my mind. We had first met in this building. . . .

"Come over here and sit down," he said, pointing to a bench. We sat down, but John was behaving strangely. We carried on an inane and pointless conversation for a few minutes, then I stood up and told him I was hungry.

"No, sit down," he said, practically pulling me down next to him. He seemed overwhelmed, nervous, and more than a little stressed, but he still didn't say anything out of the ordinary.

"John, I'm not kidding, I'm really hungry," I said, standing again. This time John stood too, and we moved toward the door that led into the building. As we were talking, he grabbed my arm and suddenly fell to one knee. I would have understood his next words even without reading his lips.

"Heather," he said, "I love you with all my heart, all my mind, and all my soul. I want to spend the rest of my life with you. Will you marry me?"

"Yes." I was too excited to cry.

John pulled a ring from his pocket and gently slid it onto my finger.

We didn't set a date right away. We knew God wanted us to be married, but I thought it'd be too difficult to be married if I was trying to finish my college education. But we also knew that we loved each other and we didn't want to wait two or three years to marry.

After weighing all the options, we finally decided to be married on June 8, 1996. I had postponed my reentry into college because of a busy speaking schedule and the work on this book. We knew we would be able to enjoy an adjustment period and finish the book before God led us in a new direction and down a different path. However, I am committed to finishing my college education.

In April 1996, during our engagement, *People* magazine came calling to do an interview on us. The people featured in *People* have usually accomplished something distinctive or unusual—they're famous, or they've just been found guilty of bigamy, or they've built the world's largest house out of tin cans, etc.

So why did *People* want to interview me six months after I had surrendered my title? Because John and I *weren't* sleeping together. Funny, isn't it, what people consider newsworthy?

The article, "Cut to the Chaste," described our courtship and engagement. "In an age when gen-X values occasionally can make even Melrose Place seem realistic, Whitestone, 23, and McCallum, 26, are proudly anachronistic," reported the article. "They are both born-again Christians for whom 'going to bed' still means getting some sleep."

When I had first begun to think about boys in my junior and senior years of high school, I spent a lot of time dreaming about my future husband. I would love him, I knew, and I wanted to offer him all of myself, body, heart, and mind. So even though many teenagers in my high school were having sex, I decided I'd keep myself pure. I even wanted to save my kisses for my future husband.

I know that many people will think I am hopelessly old-fashioned. Truthfully, I know I've led a rather sheltered life. A lot of the nasty reality of daily life doesn't penetrate my mostly silent world. I miss most off-color jokes on television and in movies, and I don't usually overhear rude people in restaurants and shopping malls.

I've been sheltered in other ways too. I didn't begin dating steadily until my first year of college, but I knew kids around me were drinking and having sex. I decided I didn't want those things in my life.

In high school I read *The Dating Dilemma* by Bob Stone and Bob Palmer. From reading that book I learned that God made us male and female, and gifted us with sexual desires. Desire is not sinful, but the misuse of sex is wrong. God wants us to wait until marriage for sex, because then men and women can enjoy it fully, without guilt, fear, or the threat of disease.

In the Bible I read that love displays good manners. "Love is patient and kind. Love is not jealous or boastful or proud or rude. Love does not demand its own way. Love is not irritable, and it keeps no record of when it has been wronged. It is never glad about injustice but rejoices whenever the truth wins out. Love never gives up, never loses faith, is always hopeful, and endures through every circumstance" (1 Corinthians 13: 4–7).

I wanted the most perfect kind of love possible.

That's why I asked David Bush, my prom date, to help me keep my promise of purity. That's why it took me six months to kiss John. And that's why we decided not to have sex before marriage.

After falling in love with John, I knew I was ready for a serious commitment. The "get your education, establish a career" mind-set wasn't necessarily the right philosophy for me to follow. Somehow I'd picked up the idea that becoming someone's wife before you'd established a career meant you couldn't be smart or successful.

But if God led me to marry John, how could I doubt the wisdom of God's plan? Each of us holds the power of influence in our hands. Even more than politicians, we can shape the future of America because we can shape its children. I think the opportunity to influence a child—who may, in turn, influence thousands of others—is an incredible task.

I would not be where I am without the efforts and dedication of my mother. I would not love and appreciate nature if it had not been for my father's influence. And, like the ripples in a lake when a pebble is tossed into it, those rings spread out into eternity, influencing only God knows how many others.

In my Bible study I recently realized that God spoke to Abram (who later became Abraham) and promised him a son, then waited twenty-five years to bestow that son upon Abraham. Why did he wait? Not only to prepare Abram to be a father to Isaac, but to prepare Abram to be the father of a nation: the nation of Israel. Sometimes when God seems to be silent regarding our future, he is preparing us—teaching us to wait, to grow in faith, in hope, and in love.

I don't know what my future holds. As I look at my life, I know that my being a celebrity might have influenced some people, but eventually the world will forget what I said and did as Miss America. But my family—the one I establish with John—will always remember the heritage I bequeath to them. I want future generations to remember my good advice, but most of all I want them to remember my love. That's the kind of influence I long for.

10 My Heart Learns to Dance Again

"*H*eather, how do you measure success?"

Someone asked that question as I was working on this book. The question caught me by surprise, and I had to stop and search for an answer.

At twenty-three I had achieved a lot of what the world calls "success": I had made good grades in school, I was an accomplished ballerina, I had learned to hear and talk on the telephone, I won preliminary pageants four times before I won Miss America. As Miss America I was given enough awards, honors, and commendations to fill an entire room. I traveled from sea to shining sea, I drove a flashy late-model sports car. But there was a time when the thought of all those accomplishments would depress me. None of those things came easily, and I paid a price for all of them. When I stopped to consider my sacrifices of time and freedom, those things didn't seem like benefits, they felt more like iron weights around my neck. The more I accomplished, the more responsible I felt to the people who were looking at me as a role model.

How do I measure success? There is really only one way. All the things I have managed to accomplish are worthwhile if they allowed or enabled me to touch other people's lives with good things. With truth. Love. Honesty. And hope.

During my year as Miss America, I was so tired and busy, I was often blind to my effect upon others. From letters and comments, I know now that I did make an impact, but I couldn't see it then. And now that I am no longer Miss America, I know I can continue to touch lives by balancing my inner life of faith with the work God calls me to do.

The night I surrendered my title, God told me he wasn't finished with me, and scarcely a month had passed before I realized there were still many doors God wanted to lead me through. In late November, just two months after I crowned Shawntel Smith Miss America 1996, I put on a flight suit and took off from the Wright-Patterson Air Force Base in an F-16 fighter jet. The one-hour flight, courtesy of the 178th Fighter Group (Ohio Air National Guard) unit at Springfield, Ohio, was part of an experiment designed to test the "active noise reduction helmet" which filters outside sound so pilots can hear the radio over the powerful roar of the jet's engines. This "noise reduction" technology will not only help pilots, but could be helpful in the future design of hearing aids.

Not only did I help fly the F-16, but while I was at Wright-Patterson AFB I met with disabled children from the greater Dayton area and participated in a question-and-answer session. I was beginning to see that Miss America wasn't the end of my dream journey—the work I had begun under the auspices of the crown might well continue. Perhaps God might still use me to help bridge the gap between the hearing and deaf worlds. I was still committed to follow his plan for my life, no matter where the path might lead.

I sacrificed many things to be Miss America—my time, my

life, my privacy. But John began to encourage me to regain the things I'd lost. He reminded me how important it was to set aside daily time for fellowship with God, to read my Bible, and to concentrate upon prayer. And he reminded me that love was the answer to overcoming any and all who came against me. Rather than praying for my critics to fail, I was to pray for their success. Perhaps, through my example and God's unconditional love, they would see my heart and know that I want only God's best for deaf people, for *all* people. . . .

From 1 Corinthians 13, I learned that if I could speak perfectly with my lips and sign beautifully with my hands but didn't love others, I would only be making meaningless noise and empty signals. And if I had the gift of wisdom and knew all the mysteries of the universe and could solve every problem about deafness and disabilities but didn't love others, my insights would be worthless. And if I had the gift of faith so that I could speak to the blind and deaf and make them see and hear, without love I would be no good to anybody. If I poured out my life to the disabled and danced before kings and presidents, I could boast about it, but if I didn't love others, I would be of no value whatsoever.

Not long ago I spoke again at the Green Valley Elementary School. I'm a former Miss America now, and I truly thought that perhaps some of the "glitter" had worn off my reputation. Since I wasn't the current Miss America, I didn't expect the students to be nearly as excited at my arrival.

I was wrong. One little boy in the class I visited blushed and told me, "I don't believe men should faint, but I am fainting!"

God is showing me that you don't have to be a Miss America to touch lives. You touch lives with your love, with your willingness to make a difference.

By the time I had finished my year as Miss America, I had learned that though I gave my time, my talent, my health, and my strength, if I did it just as a job, it meant nothing. I had to do it because I honestly loved the children who waited to see me, the young girls who yearned for a role model, the middle-aged man with a hearing problem who longed to find a steady job, the mother who wondered if her deaf son would ever succeed in school. I had to love all of them, or my work as Miss America meant nothing. I was just a smiling face, a clean-cut girl in a business suit with a rhinestone crown pinned on the lapel.

But if I could show God's love, I was offering something more priceless than diamonds, more precious than the stars above. . . .

A Diamond in the Rough

At the beginning of the year I felt that the Miss America crown was like a rough-hewn diamond I'd found in the river. I'd been given a valuable and rare stone, but what was I going to make of it? I wasn't sure. I had to do some cutting, I had to polish it and chip away more than a few rough edges. Above all, I had to be willing to allow my emerging diamond to be scrutinized and examined for the tiniest imperfections. And through all the cutting, polishing, and examining, I had to be willing to shine and reflect the light that came to me from above.

John once sent me a fax in which he quoted Oswald Chambers's *My Utmost for His Highest:* "The people who influence us most are not those who buttonhole us and talk to us, but those who live their lives like the stars in heaven and the lilies in the field, perfectly simply and unaffectedly. Those are the lives that mold us."

I was praying that I would reflect God's glorious light when I accepted an invitation to dance in the Christmas production at Robert Schuller's Crystal Cathedral. I danced ballet to "The First Noel," one of my favorite classical Christmas songs. That experience made me feel like I was in heaven. I did not have to think or analyze or fret about anything, I simply moved my body and danced in praise to God, just like those nights when I had pirouetted around the Christmas tree as a child.

After Christmas, John and I began seriously to plan our wedding. The date was set for June eighth, and we were married on St. Simons Island, a small island off the coast of Georgia. The ceremony was held in Christ Church, which was built in the 1800s, and was a small, private affair for close friends and family members. After the beautiful ceremony we changed into casual clothes and rode away on a bicycle built for two!

We honeymooned on Nevis, and I can honestly say that week was the happiest, most relaxing week I'd known in the previous two years! I have a special feeling for the beach, and John and I enjoyed our private time together. It was a wonderful way to begin a marriage.

As we relaxed, I took time to consider the choices I'd made. Some women might not have agreed with my decision to marry at age twenty-three, but I've decided to measure my success by the degree to which I've touched people for eternity. What will really matter when my life is done? I've wondered about that a lot now that my time as Miss America is over. I don't know what tomorrow holds, but I know I have a chance to join my efforts with my husband's. Together, John and I can do more to influence people in a positive way than either of us could do alone. Marriage is, after all, a partnership.

But I want people to know that the main reason for this book is to encourage others to look for positive things. I know most people will always respect me as one of the Miss America sorority, so when I speak I want to celebrate the uplifting things in life. I missed too many priceless opportunities as Miss

America when I closed my eyes and decided to nurse my own hurt, anger, and depression. I shouldn't have done that—and neither should you.

Today's opportunities will never come again. But we can't spend our lives regretting the past, for today's moment is as golden as yesterday's—if we will reach out and take it.

The Daily Prescription for Life

My Miss America platform was the STARS program (develop a positive attitude, believe in your dreams, work hard, face your weaknesses and obstacles, and build a dependable support team). Though I still believe those five points will work well for students and people striving to overcome a disability of any sort, there were dark days during my Miss America year when I was too exhausted to summon up a positive attitude, my dream-come-true was draining me, I was working very, very hard, and my weaknesses and obstacles seemed completely overwhelming. I needed something new, a different philosophy, new answers to the challenges life had brought my way.

After much prayer, thought, and discussion with Christian friends, I designed another five-point program called "The Daily Prescription for Life," which is represented by the letters TDPFL. I developed this five-point program to honor God. I don't want you to think that I always follow these points perfectly; because I'm human, I make mistakes. But God is perfect, and he never fails. And the following five principles have sprung from God's word:

1. *Take time to be quiet.* Even if you have to get up early or stay up a little later, take time for yourself. Set aside time for prayer and/or meditation. If you find yourself saying "I don't have time," readjust your priorities, because we have all been

given twenty-four hours in a day. Life is too short to spend it on the urgent while *important* things slide by unnoticed. The experience of being crowned Miss America seems like yesterday, but it was nearly three years ago. So find time to reflect. Take a walk outside, lock yourself in a closet, put down your busywork and close your eyes. Think . . . and pray.

2. *Don't forget to dream.* Rodgers and Hammerstein said it right: "If you don't have a dream, how ya gonna have a dream come true?" No matter how boring or humdrum you think your job is, take time to dream about how you can make it better. Some of my dreams were fantastic, others were more practical. I dreamed of dancing before a cheering crowd, I dreamed of a warm home of my own, I dreamed of a husband who would love me, I dreamed of cuddling with a dog. But I still dream of continuing to influence other people's lives to make a difference, to touch their hearts. I know money and fame won't make a difference. But my heart can touch others. Yours can too.

3. *Populate your life with positive people.* Think of the tiny acorn that grows to be a mighty tree. Positive people plant a tiny seed of faith that grows to be a dream fulfilled. Water makes a tree grow, and water is the love and respect you have for yourself. Positive people spread the fertilizer of encouragement! They will build you up, they will urge you to reach for the stars and grow taller! Negativism is like a cold—too easily caught and spread around. Positive attitudes are just as contagious, but they require a little extra effort!

   I love another saying of Helen Keller's: "Keep your face to the sunshine and you cannot see the shadow." Remember, while you're populating your life with positive people, look for the positive yourself!

4. *Forgive the hurt and anger of the past.* I believe a lack of forgiveness is the number one problem facing most people today. We blame others for our own faults, we are quick to point a finger at those who have hurt us. I learned that I had to stop blaming others for my upsets and start forgiving, because joy could not live in a bitter heart. Forgiveness means giving up the right to be angry or to retaliate against someone who has hurt you. Without forgiveness, the weed of anger will take over the garden of your heart and choke out joy, love, and peace. Go to the person who has hurt you and offer your forgiveness. If they don't accept it, at least you'll have done what you ought to do. Forget about the past and move forward.

Helen Keller also had something to say about moving on. "When one door of happiness closes," she once said, "another opens, but often we look so long at the closed door that we do not see the one which has been opened for us."

Forget the hurts and disappointments of your past, and look ahead. You might be amazed at the doors God is willing to open for you, if you will only listen to his voice . . . with your heart.

5. *Love yourself as God loves you.* One of the little girls who wrote to me said she'd heard that a person couldn't love himself and God too, but there's a difference between selfishly serving ourselves and understanding that God holds us in great esteem. I didn't love myself very much when I was Miss America. I was hurt by other people's criticism. Though thousands of people told me nice things, I remembered the negatives. I didn't please everyone, and so I thought I had completely failed. I felt hurt . . . and angry. Because people don't like being around negative people, I didn't like being around myself.

Then John came into my life and he reminded me that Jesus loved me. And, in time, I saw that John loved me. And even though I didn't feel worthy of that love—I couldn't even believe in it at first—I learned to trust. And both God and John were faithful. They gave me a precious gift: my self-esteem.

Deaf Issues Overseas

In early 1996, right before John and I were married, I was invited to travel to Taiwan and speak about deaf issues. I had never been to Asia, and so was thrilled to have the opportunity to travel overseas. My trip was sponsored by Citibank's "With Your Heart You Can Hear the Whole World" charity drive, and the bank worked with the Taipei city government to promote early detection and intervention programs. As I walked through the buildings and schools of Taipei, I was greeted with the universal "I love you" sign that made me feel at home.

Taiwan is an extremely modern and beautiful country, but when I entered the deaf community there, I felt as though I had traveled back to the nineteenth century. The prevailing cultural opinion holds that deaf people cannot have a normal life, and so few deaf Taiwanese people have more than a second-grade education. I visited one deaf school that did have computers, but the students were playing games with them, not really learning how to speak. I asked if they had learned to write, and was told that the deaf students were treated as if they were learning-impaired.

I was shocked. I talked about my STARS program (an interpreter signed for the audience), but the students looked at me blankly as if they didn't understand. Then I asked, "How many of you have heard of Helen Keller?" and out of five hundred students only three or four raised their hands.

They had no role models! I was nearly speechless with surprise. Since surrendering my title, I have been involved with
the Helen Keller Eye Research Foundation of Birmingham, Alabama, and I believe all deaf and blind people should be acquainted with her story. Later during that trip I spoke in a
public high school for hearing girls, and when I asked how
many had heard of Helen Keller, nearly every girl raised her
hand. Why didn't the deaf students—who desperately needed
her example—know about Helen Keller?

Just thinking about that oversight made my heart race.
Helen Keller had been my role model my entire life, her example had given me hope. So many of her inspiring quotes had
encouraged me to strive for my dreams.

I soon began to understand why none of the deaf Taiwanese
students had heard of Helen Keller. They are still living in an
age that considers deafness nearly as great an obstacle to learning as mental retardation; they couldn't seem to stop marveling
over the fact that I was a living, thinking, rational human
being. During one question-and-answer session a high school
girl stood up and asked, "Do you think you will have a normal
marriage?"

Nonplussed, I answered, "My husband looks at me as a person, not as a disability."

To their credit, many people in Taiwan are striving to
change things. I met one mother, Joanna Nichols, who had
gone to the United States to learn about education for deaf
people. Taking responsibility for her deaf daughter's education,
she has studied cued speech, acoupedics, sign language, and
oral speech. She is trying to make a difference not only for her
daughter but for all deaf children. With the help of Citibank,
she was instrumental in arranging my visit to Taiwan.

Many parents with deaf children today have high expectations for them. I am concerned that parents who see or hear

me may think their children capable of immediate speech. I want to give parents hope, but that hope should be tempered with realism. I did not speak very well when I was little. It took me six years to learn how to say my last name correctly. In language skills I have always lagged far behind my age level.

I hope parents will not expect their deaf children to speak well and use perfect English grammar when they are young. Maturity will bring progress, and your hard work will bring results. Just don't expect too much too soon. Enjoy every moment with your children because life is short. God has not given you this precious child in order to put you to work twenty-four hours a day. God has given you this deaf child because he or she needs your love. Children hunger for love more than success.

One quote has never lost its power to move me: "Some people complain because God put thorns on roses, while others praise him for putting roses among thorns." How true that is! We must learn to recognize and praise God for the good things he has brought into our lives.

That was the message I took to the people of Taiwan. They were lovely; no one could be more generous or gracious. The girls in the public high school brought me flowers and a teddy bear, and they were eager to practice their English with me. I felt so much respect, love, and warm kindness. They wanted to hear my speech, they wanted to know about my then-fiancé, they wanted to know about being Miss America. One girl, however, stumped me with her question. She asked: "If you could hear for one day, what would you do?"

I was caught unprepared, so on the spur of the moment I replied that I'd probably try to hear as many unfamiliar words as I could, because it's hard to use new vocabulary correctly when you can't hear them being pronounced.

But today, if asked the same question, I'd probably reply that I'd spend the day on the beach with John, just listening to his precious voice. Matters of the heart are now more precious to me than matters of the mind.

Life is a journey, and God directs the person who asks for his help . . . and follows his dream. He allowed me to become deaf, and I'm grateful for his wisdom. Being deaf taught me to be disciplined, and then my heart taught me to dance.

If I hadn't learned discipline and dance, I would never have entered a pageant . . . and won.

If I hadn't been Miss America, I would never have met John. Neither would I be writing this book.

I can't second-guess God. If I could be anyone I wanted to be, I would be Heather Whitestone McCallum. I'm happy being who God called me to be. I still have dreams—I'd love to learn ice dancing, and I'd love to dance more regularly—but my life belongs to God. I'll follow where he leads.

About the Author

HEATHER WHITESTONE was born and raised in Alabama. She attended the Central Institute for the Deaf in St. Louis and later graduated from her hometown high school. While in college, Heather dedicated herself to competing in local pageants. After coming in second for two years, she won the Miss Alabama Pageant in 1995 and a few months later became Miss America. Since relinquishing her title she has crossed the country motivating corporate, civic, and religious organizations. She was married in June 1996 and now lives in Atlanta, Georgia, with her husband, John McCallum.

ANGELA ELWELL HUNT is the author of the best-selling *The Tale of Three Trees*. She and her family live in Florida.

Photo Credits

Photos #6, 11, 12, 19, 20 copyright © 1994, 1995 C. P. News, J. M. Frank. Used with permission of the Miss America Organization.

Photo #7 copyright © 1994 A. P. Wide World Photos.

Photo #14 copyright © 1994 *The Oregonian*.

Photo #27 copyright © 1996 Bill Adler.

All other photos are the property of the author.